New Daylight

CW01674569

Edited by **Gordon Giles** **January–April 2026**

BRF Ministries
15 The Chambers, Vineyard,
Abingdon OX14 3FE
+44 (0)1865 319700 | brf.org.uk

Bible Reading Fellowship is a charity (233280) and company limited by guarantee (301324), registered in England and Wales

EU Authorised Representative: Easy Access System Europe –
Mustamäe tee 50, 10621 Tallinn, Estonia, **gpsr.requests@easproject.com**

ISBN 978 1 80039 477 3

Cover photo by pexels.com/@ron-lach

Distributed in Australia by:
MediaCom Education Inc, PO Box 610, Unley, SA 5061
Tel: 1 800 811 311 | admin@mediacom.org.au

Distributed in New Zealand by:
Scripture Union Wholesale, PO Box 760, Wellington 6140
Tel: 04 385 0421 | suwholesale@clear.net.nz

Acknowledgements
Scripture quotations marked with the following abbreviations are taken from the version shown. Where no abbreviation is given, the quotation is taken from the same version as the headline reference. NIV: The Holy Bible, New International Version, Anglicised edition, copyright © 1979, 1984, 2011 by Biblica. Used by permission of Hodder & Stoughton Publishers, an Hachette UK company. All rights reserved. 'NIV' is a registered trademark of Biblica. UK trademark number 1448790. ESV: The Holy Bible, English Standard Version, published by HarperCollins Publishers, © 2001 Crossway Bibles, a division of Good News Publishers. Used by permission. All rights reserved. NRSV: the New Revised Standard Version Updated Edition. Copyright © 2021 National Council of Churches of Christ in the United States of America. Used by permission. All rights reserved worldwide.

A catalogue record for this book is available from the British Library

Printed and bound in the UK by Zenith Media NP4 0DQ

Suggestions for using *New Daylight*

Find a regular time and place, if possible, where you can read and pray undisturbed. Before you begin, take time to be still and perhaps use the prayer of BRF Ministries on page 6. Then read the Bible passage slowly (try reading it aloud if you find it overfamiliar), followed by the comment. You can also use *New Daylight* for group study and discussion, if you prefer.

The prayer or point for reflection can be a starting point for your own meditation and prayer. Many people like to keep a journal to record their thoughts about a Bible passage and items for prayer. In *New Daylight* we also note the Sundays and some special festivals from the church calendar, to keep in step with the Christian year.

New Daylight and the Bible

New Daylight contributors use a range of Bible versions, and you will find a list of the versions used opposite. You are welcome to use your own preferred version alongside the passage printed in the notes. This can be particularly helpful if the Bible text has been abridged.

New Daylight affirms that the whole of the Bible is God's revelation to us, and we should read, reflect on and learn from every part of both Old and New Testaments. Usually the printed comment presents a straightforward 'thought for the day', but sometimes it may also raise questions rather than simply providing answers, as we wrestle with some of the more difficult passages of scripture.

New Daylight is also available in a compact size edition. Visit your local Christian bookshop or BRF's online shop brfonline.org.uk. To obtain an audio version for the blind or partially sighted, contact Torch Trust for the Blind, Torch House, Torch Way, Northampton Road, Market Harborough LE16 9HL; +44 (0)1858 438260; info@torchtrust.org.

Comment on *New Daylight*

To send feedback, please email enquiries@brf.org.uk, phone **+44 (0)1865 319700** or write to the address shown opposite.

Writers in this issue

Amanda Bloor is archdeacon of Cleveland in the diocese of York, and has previously been a bishop's chaplain, a diocesan director of ordinands, an advisor in women's ministry and a parish priest.

Amy Boucher Pye is a London-based writer, speaker and spiritual director. She is the author of several books, including *Holding onto Hope* (BRF Ministries, 2023). Find her at **amyboucherpye.com**.

Ruth Hassall is a speaker, trainer and coach on issues of leadership and discipleship. She is the author of *Growing Young Leaders: A practical guide to mentoring teens* (BRF Ministries, 2022).

Margot Hodson is theology and education director for the John Ray Initiative and a vicar in the Oxford diocese. **Martin Hodson** is a plant scientist and environmental biologist and teaches at both universities in Oxford. They are the authors of *A Christian Guide to Environmental Issues* (BRF Ministries, 2021).

Tony Horsfall is an author, retreat leader and mentor. Among his many books published with BRF Ministries are *Attentive to God*, *Knowing You, Jesus*, *Working from a Place of Rest*, *Rhythms of Grace* and *Grief Notes*.

Martin Leckebusch worked in IT for 37 years before retiring to spend more time writing. He lives in Gloucester, is an elder at a Baptist church, and is the author of over 500 published hymn texts.

Roland Riem is vice-dean of Winchester Cathedral, where he is involved in the greening of the cathedral and the development of its interpretation for visitors.

Naomi Starkey is honorary canon and vicar (Ministry Area Leader) of Bro Eryri, six church communities in the shadow of Yr Wyddfa (Snowdon) in north Wales. She is a former editor of *New Daylight*.

Sheila Walker is a former associate priest serving with rural churches in Oxfordshire and Devon, and author of *Contemporary Reflections*, together with an eclectic mix of poems, study notes and children's stories.

Catherine Williams is an Anglican priest working as a spiritual director and freelance writer. She is the lead voice on the Church of England's *Daily Prayer* and *Time to Pray* apps.

Gordon Giles writes...

Welcome to a new year and a new edition of *New Daylight*. We begin – as we always do – in the Christmas season and traverse the three peaks of Epiphany and the slopes of Lent before descending to the depths of Holy Week, and are then raised up through Easter Week and beyond.

The three 'peaks' of Epiphany are the three miracles of revealing – the *tribus miraculum* – the visit of the Magi, the baptism of Jesus and the changing of water into wine, the first of Jesus' miracles, according to John. This undulating journey connects Christmas with Easter in a way that secular or commercial enterprises do not realise or recognise.

Or do they? In December 2024 Aldi supermarkets started selling a 'Chreaster Egg'. These chocolate eggs inevitably drew media attention. Ecclesiastical eyebrows were raised, and I even tried one in front of TV cameras. So yes, dear reader, I am now a media chocolate taster! I was even quoted in *The Daily Telegraph*, a publication with an international reach almost as great as *New Daylight*...

Joking aside, the fuss was all about pairing Christmas with Easter. This is hardly original or new, and is an extension of the chocolatisation of Christianity (think of Valentine's Day and Halloween as well as Easter). For the wood of the manger is the wood of the cross; one cannot have one without the other, and each only makes sense, theologically, redemptively and pastorally, alongside the other. The Word made flesh was born to die, and rise again for our justification. Cover it in chocolate if you must, but the bittersweet centre is the loving mercy of God, incarnate at Christmas, revealed at Epiphany and raised twice in Holy Week: first on the cross and secondly from the empty tomb.

This is our faith and the message to be proclaimed to the world. St Francis may have said, 'Preach the gospel. If necessary, use words.' In today's religiously illiterate culture we might say, 'Preach the gospel. If necessary, use chocolate.'

As you read this edition of *New Daylight*, travel from Christmas to Easter. Taste the journey, and remember that Easter eggs point us backwards to Christmas too.

GORDON GILES

The prayer of BRF Ministries

Faithful God,
thank you for growing BRF
from small beginnings
into the worldwide family of BRF Ministries.
We rejoice as young and old
discover you through your word
and grow daily in faith and love.
Keep us humble in your service,
ambitious for your glory
and open to new opportunities.
For your name's sake,
Amen.

'It is such a joy to be part of this amazing project'

As part of our BRF Resources ministry, we're raising funds to give away copies of Bible reading notes and other resources to those who aren't able to access them any other way, working with food banks and chaplaincy services, in prisons, hospitals and care homes.

'This very generous gift will be hugely appreciated, and truly bless each recipient… Bless you for your kindness.'

'We would like to send our enormous thanks to all involved. Your generosity will have a significant impact and will help us to continue to provide support to local people in crisis, and for this we cannot thank you enough.'

If you've enjoyed and benefited from our resources, would you consider paying it forward to enable others to do so too?

Make a gift at **brf.org.uk/donate**

Genesis 1—4

Happy New Year! Where better to start a new year than in the opening chapters of Genesis, the beginning of all things? Much may be familiar in these passages, yet they continue to offer new insights as well as raising questions for 21st-century believers. These chapters remain important, because they carry some of the Bible's key teaching on the origins of the universe, life and evil. Any biblically based approach to morality or ethics has to take note of what is said here.

Some of the conundrums from Genesis arise from the kind of document it is. We do not know who first put these accounts in writing or how stories shared by word of mouth were gathered to become the document we now have. Yet someone felt these were worth writing down, preserving and passing on to future generations (eventually including ours).

When these accounts were first recorded, they were written by and for people whose culture was very different from our own. We need to bear this in mind as we read. To imagine that those authors or editors intended to write a scientific explanation of the world's beginnings would be a huge mistake – such an approach would have been utterly alien to their thinking. Science explores 'how' things happen; Genesis is more concerned with 'why' and with 'who' made them happen.

Similarly, our authors can hardly have intended to write 'history' in the sense of today's historians, with sources dutifully compared and cross-referenced in an effort to be accurate and objective. This account of life's origins focuses on the relationships of the key characters, including the creator; it is these which stand out, along with their implications for the reader.

Nevertheless, we need not feel daunted as we approach these chapters. The Spirit of God, whose activity is noted here, was at work alongside the human authors, shaping their writing. He also works to enlighten us as we read. As we study Genesis 1—4, it may be helpful to keep in mind a few basic questions: what did these authors – human and divine – want to teach us about ourselves as human beings? About how we should relate to one another? About the world we inhabit? And about the God who made everything?

MARTIN LECKEBUSCH

And God said…

In the beginning God created the heavens and the earth. Now the earth was formless and empty, darkness was over the surface of the deep, and the Spirit of God was hovering over the waters. And God said, 'Let there be light,' and there was light. God saw that the light was good, and he separated the light from the darkness. God called the light 'day', and the darkness he called 'night'. And there was evening, and there was morning – the first day.

The stories told in these chapters – the cosmic story, and in due course the human story within it – begin with God. He is announced as being 'there' at the beginning, although paradoxically there was neither a place to call 'there' nor a time to call 'then'. God is presented as being beyond both these ideas. However, the narrator writes in ways suitable for finite human beings to understand from their perspective within time and space.

In part, the story told here resembles ancient accounts from other cultures exploring the world's origins. Scholars tell us that one feature found among those stories was the need to bring order to a scene of chaos; here, too, is a description of darkness, depth and emptiness. Yet God had plans to form better things. The Spirit of God hovered over what was shapeless and uncontrolled, apparently planning what was to be.

The creation itself begins (and in subsequent stages is largely continued) with God speaking: 'And God said…' All through the Bible, God is revealed as the one who speaks, and in particular in such power that things are brought into being by his decree. That begins here with the creation of light, and the light was good. Interestingly, the darkness is not totally obliterated by the light, but is restricted; it is then harnessed to fulfil a role in the created order. Under God's sovereign control, it finds its proper place.

This opening phase of creation – the first day, so the beginning of what we call 'time' – gives us an initial glimpse of God's creative imagination and power. Pause to consider these and to worship.

Majestic Creator, you were before all things,
and all things owe you their existence. We praise you. Amen.

MARTIN LECKEBUSCH

Let there be... And it was so

And God said, 'Let there be a vault between the waters...' And it was so. God called the vault 'sky'. And there was evening, and there was morning – the second day. And God said, 'Let... dry ground appear... Let the land produce vegetation... Let there be lights in... the sky to separate the day from the night, and... to give light on the earth'... He also made the stars... And God said, 'Let the water teem with living creatures, and let birds fly above the earth...' God blessed them and said, 'Be fruitful and increase in number...' And there was evening, and there was morning... And God said, 'Let the land produce living creatures according to their kinds: the livestock, the creatures that move along the ground, and the wild animals...' And it was so... And God saw that it was good.

As the account of creation unfolds a poetic rhythm shapes the narrative. Four repeated phrases stand out.

First, 'And God said...' As we recalled yesterday, creation owes its existence to God and his intention to make a cosmos. His purposefulness is revealed in what he designed, and in how he brought order to what was random and unformed.

Second, 'And it was so.' We have also already noted the Bible's stress on the power of God's creative word – what he says is done. Yet there are hints that he is more deeply involved in the processes of creation. 'He also made the stars' may imply a more active engagement than merely issuing commands. Our increasing knowledge of the immense forces, distances and complexities involved should further prompt our praise.

The third poetic phrase is 'There was evening, and... morning', as one by one creation's days are counted off. There is a sense of steady work bringing meaning and control; chaos is superseded by God's handiwork.

This is reflected in the final phrase to echo through this opening chapter: 'God saw that it was good.' We can have confidence in the kindness and care of the one who planned, created, furnished and still sustains our planetary home.

Lord God, thank you for creating such a beautiful world and such a fine, intricate universe. Amen.

MARTIN LECKEBUSCH

In his own image

Then God said, 'Let us make mankind in our image, in our likeness, so that they may rule over the fish in the sea and the birds in the sky, over the livestock and all the wild animals, and over all the creatures that move along the ground.' So God created mankind in his own image, in the image of God he created them; male and female he created them. God blessed them and said to them, 'Be fruitful and increase in number; fill the earth and subdue it. Rule over… every living creature… I give you every seed-bearing plant… and every tree that has fruit with seed in it… for food'… God saw all that he had made, and it was very good. And there was evening, and there was morning – the sixth day.

Day six sees the creation of humans, with particular detail about the role of these created beings. First, humans bear the image of God, which is not said of anything else God made. This is reflected in the 'male and female' aspect of humans: both equally carry the likeness of their creator.

While the author does not spell out what is meant by 'in our image', there is at least a hint in what follows: the responsibility of ruling over other creatures. In this, the human creatures represent God within his world. There is also a sense that humans are answerable to God, for although they are to fill and subdue the earth there are limitations on their actions, such as what they may eat. We should consider ourselves charged to care for the world around us, not given free rein to maltreat it.

Finally, here alone does God affirm his handiwork as 'very' good. This relates to 'all' he had made, rather than to humans alone. Their arrival completes and crowns the initial creative programme, but the world is not purely for their pleasure or benefit. It is worth pondering that humans were made on the same day as the other land animals – yes, they bear God's image, but they are firmly positioned as creatures within the created order.

God our maker, forgive our selfish misuse of your creation and teach us to handle it wisely, to honour you. Amen.

MARTIN LECKEBUSCH

The seventh day

God saw all that he had made, and it was very good. And there was evening, and there was morning – the sixth day. Thus the heavens and the earth were completed in all their vast array. By the seventh day God had finished the work he had been doing; so on the seventh day he rested from all his work. Then God blessed the seventh day and made it holy, because on it he rested from all the work of creating that he had done.

An RE teacher once announced to her class, 'God created the world in seven days,' to which my daughter, one of her students, simply said, 'Six.' The teacher thought, and accepted the correction!

The point was well made. The steady, powerful activity which had brought everything into being was complete; the result was not a static universe but one in which each component was in its proper place and rhythm. The 'very good' creation provided for the needs of its inhabitants, human and animal. The balanced interplay of ecosystems did not inhibit change, but allowed it while offering a restful completeness which did not require constant, frantic attention. The seventh day therefore became a time for relaxation.

Setting the seventh day apart as 'holy' marked this. It also framed the seventh day as one for worship rather than work, a theme further developed later in the biblical story. The seventh day becomes a day for grateful recognition and trusting acceptance of God's provision.

Today's 24/7 society runs at odds with this whole approach to life. Its model sees the world as something to be exploited at every opportunity. The drive to acquire more does not sit well with 'unproductive' periods. It has become countercultural to set aside time for reflecting on God's generosity and the inherent goodness and beauty of his handiwork. Yet to do so is also profoundly healthy: physically, mentally and spiritually. Even where outside pressures or calls for compassion demand activity, it is vital for us to pause regularly – just as God himself did.

Most Christians treat Sunday (rather than Saturday, the 'seventh day') as their day for rest – yet many are busier than ever on that day. Could you make today more restful and worshipful?

Teach me, Lord, to honour your holiness with my life's rhythms. Amen.

MARTIN LECKEBUSCH

Home and work

The Lord God formed a man from the dust of the ground and breathed into his nostrils the breath of life, and the man became a living being. Now the Lord God had planted a garden in the east, in Eden, and… made all kinds of trees grow… that were pleasing to the eye and good for food. In the middle of the garden were the tree of life and the tree of the knowledge of good and evil… The Lord God took the man and put him in the Garden of Eden to work it and take care of it. And the Lord God commanded the man, 'You are free to eat from any tree in the garden; but you must not eat from the tree of the knowledge of good and evil, for when you eat of it you will certainly die.'

These verses start to explore in more detail what life was like for the newly created humans. First we see God's careful attention: the concept of the Lord shaping soil then breathing life into it is tender and homely. We also see something of his provision for these creatures. The whole world had been furnished with abundant plant life, but Eden was apparently given special care. This was neither field nor forest but a garden, deliberately cultivated to be a pleasant and welcoming home for these new people.

Yet Eden was also to be a place of work. In practice, the responsibility to 'subdue' the earth involved actual labour: caring for creation would mean thoughtful, deliberate action. To be human and made in God's image includes purposeful activity. This was not meant to be a struggle to wrestle benefit from a reluctant environment; abundant good food was provided. Yet nor was life in God's image, in God's garden, an endless holiday.

Another aspect of being human is choice. The species of the 'tree of knowledge' is irrelevant; what matters is that God wanted a relationship in which responsible humans would willingly do as he said. Without the freedom to choose, human existence would be diminished, but the wrong choice would bring bad and irreversible consequences.

Help me, Lord God, to see what choices matter today, especially in caring for your good creation. Amen.

MARTIN LECKEBUSCH

Two's company

The Lord God said, 'It is not good for the man to be alone. I will make a helper suitable for him.' Now the Lord God had formed... all the wild animals and all the birds in the sky. He brought them to the man to see what he would name them... But for Adam no suitable helper was found. So the Lord God caused the man to fall into a deep sleep; and... he took one of the man's ribs and then closed up the place with flesh. Then the Lord God made a woman from the rib he had taken out of the man, and he brought her to the man. The man said, 'This is now bone of my bones and flesh of my flesh; she shall be called "woman", for she was taken out of man.'

Let us recall the questions from the Introduction about what the author of Genesis and the Spirit of God want us to learn from each part of this account. What do we find out about ourselves? This story says we are social beings. Living completely in isolation is not healthy for us, no matter how much we may sometimes crave space and time alone. Unlike other aspects of creation, the man's being alone was 'not good'.

How should we relate to one another? Adam's first sight of the woman evokes a strong reaction: he recognises in her someone like himself, and in that way distinct from the creatures he named earlier. Even though he understands she is not identical to him, the 'sameness' between them as humans produces a unique bond which outweighs their differences.

How should we relate to the world we inhabit? God provoked the man's interest and curiosity by bringing all the animals to him. The task of naming them reinforced human responsibility to care for them and to rule over them.

What does this passage say about God? Once again, we see the mingling of the Lord's creative activity and his intimate care for his human creatures. By giving them each other he addressed their social and emotional needs, just as the garden he provided was to meet their physical needs.

Every human being carries your image, Lord.
Help me to see it more clearly. Amen.

MARTIN LECKEBUSCH

Deception and rebellion

Now the snake... said to the woman, 'Did God really say, "You must not eat from any tree in the garden"?' The woman said... 'God did say, "You must not eat fruit from the tree that is in the middle of the garden... or you will die."' 'You will not certainly die,' the snake said... 'you will be like God, knowing good and evil.' When the woman saw that the fruit... was... desirable for gaining wisdom, she took some and ate it. She also gave some to her husband... and he ate it. Then... they realised that they were naked... The man and his wife heard the sound of the Lord God... in the garden... and they hid... But the Lord God called to the man, 'Where are you?' He answered... 'I was afraid because I was naked; so I hid.'

Through the wily snake's scheming and the disobedience this triggered, creation's essential goodness was badly damaged. The narrator tells how this creature sowed doubt, deception and distortion to lure the first humans away from the path God had mapped out for them. This couple had been given one critical choice; the snake wanted to persuade them to choose badly. The subtlety of his method is illuminating. His initial question raises the possibility that God might be unloving in his rules and ungenerous in his provision. Then come the direct lies: 'You will not die... you will be like God.'

The irony here is that God had made human beings in his own image. In wanting to be 'like God' the woman wanted something that was effectively already hers! Yet these distortions entice the woman to look at the prohibited fruit with new eyes. The results are a disaster. The 'knowledge of good and evil' turns out to be a contaminating experience of the latter, and then the couple realise that they have done wrong.

The immediate consequences indicate fear and shame. Adam and his wife no longer feel comfortable relating to God as they had before. Yet they cannot hide and will soon find that even worse consequences follow.

God, help me to be quicker at spotting the danger of temptation – and better at remembering that you always want what is best for me. Amen.

MARTIN LECKEBUSCH

The day of reckoning

[The Lord God] said… 'Have you eaten from the tree from which I commanded you not to eat?' The man said, 'The woman… gave me some fruit… and I ate it'… The woman said, 'The snake deceived me, and I ate.' So the Lord God said to the snake… 'Cursed are you above all livestock…' To the woman he said, 'I will make your pains in childbearing very severe…' To Adam he said… 'Cursed is the ground because of you… By the sweat of your brow you will eat your food… and to dust you will return'… And the Lord God said, 'The man has now become like one of us, knowing good and evil. He must not be allowed to… take also from the tree of life and eat, and live for ever.' So the Lord God banished him from the Garden of Eden.

The questioning to which the Lord subjects the man and woman is superfluous: the creator obviously knows what has happened. Yet the human beings have to realise for themselves the enormity of their actions, so that they can admit their guilt and better understand the justice of their punishment. Another part of being human is implied here: taking responsibility for our behaviour.

The punishment they receive is wide-ranging, making life more burdensome and uncomfortable for them both, albeit in different ways. Childbearing becomes more difficult; daily work becomes toil. The decree that humans will return to dust echoes the earlier warning of death as a result of disobedience. Their relationships with God, with each other and with their environment are all affected.

Interestingly, although the snake and the ground are cursed, the man and woman are not. God still cares for them. Even expulsion from their beautiful home is for their ultimate good, because a second tree in Eden has now become dangerous. The implication is that by eating from the 'tree of life' they might somehow become permanently trapped in their rebellious state, with no hope of release.

Forgive me, Lord, when I am slow to take responsibility for my failures and my rebellion against you, and show me how I can help make this damaged world a better place. Amen.

MARTIN LECKEBUSCH

Blood brothers?

Eve… gave birth to Cain… Later she gave birth to… Abel… Abel kept flocks, and Cain worked the soil… Cain brought some… fruits of the soil as an offering to the Lord. But Abel… brought… fat portions from… his flock. The Lord looked with favour on Abel and his offering, but on Cain… he did not… So Cain was very angry… Then the Lord said… 'Why is your face downcast?… Sin is crouching at your door… you must rule over it'… While they were in the field, Cain attacked his brother Abel and killed him. Then the Lord said to Cain, 'Where is your brother Abel?'… He replied, 'Am I my brother's keeper?' The Lord said… 'Your brother's blood cries out to me from the ground. Now you are under a curse… You will be a restless wanderer…' So Cain went out from the Lord's presence.

The story moves on. The first humans become the first family when children are born. In that next generation the effects of sin become worse. It is sobering to note that the earliest human death recorded in scripture is a domestic murder.

From the narrator's perspective, the issue here is not why Abel's offering was more acceptable than Cain's, but rather how Cain handled that. His reactions begin with deep anger, lacking any apparent willingness to listen, learn and change his behaviour. Cain receives a clear warning from the Lord that he is now at an important point of choice. His failure to master sin leads to what looks like premeditated violence, conducted in the belief that he can get away with what he does. Afterwards he refuses to take any responsibility for his actions; but he cannot evade their consequences.

Once again we see pointers to what is entailed in being human. This time, though, sin's lurking presence seems threatening rather than alluring. Who among us has not felt the pressure to act out of anger, and done something we subsequently regretted? This story holds a mirror before us; if we are honest, we may see ourselves reflected here in uncomfortable ways.

Lord, sometimes sin crouches at my door; I can master it or succumb to it. Help me to be aware of those points of choice and to respond well.

MARTIN LECKEBUSCH

The downward spiral

The Lord said... 'Anyone who kills Cain will suffer vengeance seven times over...' Cain made love to his wife, and she... gave birth to Enoch. Cain was then building a city, and he named it after his son... To Enoch was born Irad... the father of Mehujael... the father of Methushael... the father of Lamech. Lamech married two women... Adah and... Zillah. Adah gave birth to Jabal... the father of those who live in tents and raise livestock. His brother's name was Jubal... the father of all who play stringed instruments and pipes. Zillah... had a son, Tubal-Cain, who forged... tools out of bronze and iron... Lamech said to his wives... 'I have killed a man for wounding me... If Cain is avenged seven times, then Lamech seventy-seven times'... At that time people began to call on the name of the Lord.

Cain's fear of suffering vengeance is assuaged by God's protective sanction, which limits retribution. After this the narrative skips selectively down the generations until Cain's sin is echoed by Lamech's actions. Yet while the penalty for anyone harming Cain was serious, without any authority Lamech stakes a claim to absurdly greater protection. Was this because of how corrupt society had become, or did he simply have too great an opinion of his own worth?

The passing of time also led to widespread developments in human life: patterns of settled living and, by contrast, of nomadic animal husbandry; in family life, polygamy; in culture, the growth of music; and through metalwork, early examples of technology. Human ingenuity and skill are reflected in these activities, but it is also possible that those pursuing them are driven by mixed motives. Cain's decision to name a city after his son, for example, implies a measure of pride. Perhaps the most telling indictment on human activity is the concluding note: people began to call on God's name, implying that for quite some time, by then, ordinary life had largely been lived without reference to God. Are things very different in today's secular societies?

Think of the various aspects of your life – your work, cultural involvement or social activity. How can you pursue these with a greater awareness of God?

Lord, I call on your name: help me live within your creation with grace, wisdom and an awareness of you. Amen.

MARTIN LECKEBUSCH

1 Corinthians 9—11

I often wonder how Paul might have written to my church – or yours! Would we welcome this kind of apostolic oversight or hesitate to open the letter for fear of being hauled over the coals? Paul's relationship with the church at Corinth could be stormy: but then, he was never one to sacrifice honesty and concern for God's honour for the sake of peace and quiet or fear of offending his hearers.

Corinth certainly posed a significant challenge: cosmopolitan, prosperous, but rough and crowded, fractious, argumentative, with a reputation for sexual licence and 'anything goes'. Plenty of modern cities could answer to such a description, and many of the challenges are equally relevant today. Although Paul is keen to affirm and encourage the Christian community, in these two chapters we find some pretty straight talking from him. Whether we are city or country dwellers, his words may resonate equally strongly with us. Human nature changes little, and we face many similar issues.

In an age of influencers, where does authority lie for us? What do we think about the whole issue of rights? How do we share our faith? What kind of spiritual disciplines are we finding helpful – that is, practices which position us so that God can transform us? Might we – perish the thought! – ever be guilty of grumbling, compromise, complacency? Just how far are we prepared to trust God? Are we truly one in Christ or a somewhat broken body? How do we approach the Lord's supper?

Of course, no church is perfect, and we are not to beat ourselves up for our shortcomings. But it is also true that God disciplines those he loves, both for our own sake, so that we may become more fully the people he created us to be, and so that, as individuals and communities, our lives may more truly honour him and reflect his love to those around us.

We therefore need that balance of challenge and affirmation, rod and staff, stick and carrot. May God grant us grace, as we read these chapters, to receive both, knowing that nothing can shake his love or his loving purposes for us.

SHEILA WALKER

Speaking with authority

Am I not free? Am I not an apostle? Have I not seen Jesus our Lord? Are not you my workmanship in the Lord? If to others I am not an apostle, at least I am to you, for you are the seal of my apostleship in the Lord. This is my defence to those who would examine me. Do we not have the right to eat and drink?

Who does he think he is, telling us what to do? Paul has not been mincing his words as he pulls the Corinthian Christians up about their conduct, and no one likes to be hauled over the coals. Hence, as so often, they respond not by addressing the issue but by attacking the messenger.

Paul is confident, though, in his calling as an apostle. The general understanding of the term is 'one who is sent with a purpose', though in the early church it came to mean those who had accompanied Christ and were witnesses of his resurrection, or those second-generation messengers sent out in turn by them. Though Paul had not been with Jesus during his ministry – far from it – his experience on the Damascus road and the subsequent years before his own ministry constituted his own legitimate experience of Jesus and his calling to the role of apostle.

If, as Jesus says, a tree is known by its fruit, then Paul's calling as an apostle is evidenced by its results: the redeemed lives of those Corinthians who have come to faith as a result of his teaching. An absence of such fruit does not necessarily disprove someone's calling; there are faithful missionaries whose labours appeared at the time to be in vain, but which provided a foundation on which others could build.

There is a challenge here about our attitude to those in authority. It is easy to mutter and criticise; it is a rare Christian leader who will not have been on the receiving end of challenge and negativity. No leader is perfect, but we are to be respectful, encouraging and prayerful towards those whom God has sent to lead us in our faith journey.

Lord, help me to take time today to encourage and pray for those to whom I look for spiritual leadership. Amen.

SHEILA WALKER

Earning a reward

Who plants a vineyard and does not eat any of its fruit? Or who tends a flock and does not get any of its milk? Do I say this on human authority? Does not the law also say the same? For it is written in the law of Moses, 'You shall not muzzle an ox while it is treading out the grain'... If we have sown spiritual things among you, is it too much if we harvest material things?

It can be a cause for concern that increasing demands for safeguarding and health-and-safety training deter many would-be volunteers – without whom much of the fabric of our community life could unravel. Should we be so dependent on volunteers? There is much to be said in favour of a loving, unselfish generosity of spirit, but also of the right for work to be rewarded.

Paul is certainly good at arguing his case for the latter. First, it is only common sense: vineyard owners or livestock farmers will naturally enjoy the benefits of their work; they will not go elsewhere for wine or milk. Second, it is all in the scriptures: it is not just the oxen that concern the Lord; this is a good principle for all workers.

Paul will go on to appeal to the Corinthians' sense of natural justice: if they have received so much spiritual blessing from him, surely it is fair for them to show their appreciation in some way? Hospitality and generosity are, after all, hallmarks of Christian character. And in Jewish worship it has long been the custom for the priests and Levites to receive a share of the sacrifices and offerings brought to the Lord. And finally, when Jesus sends out the disciples to preach and teach, he tells them to not take provisions, because those who are blessed by them should provide for them.

We hear much today about rights of various kinds. It is right to be paid a proper return for work undertaken, but it is also good to serve others in kind.

Lord, you are a God of both justice and generosity.
May we understand what these look like in your eyes. Amen.

SHEILA WALKER

Foregoing my rights

But I have made no use of any of these rights... If I proclaim the gospel, this gives me no ground for boasting, for an obligation is laid on me, and woe to me if I do not proclaim the gospel!... What then is my wage? Just this: that in my proclamation I may make the gospel free of charge, so as not to make full use of my rights in the gospel.

Having presented a cast-iron defence of his rights, Paul now confounds the Corinthian Christians by discarding it completely. For him, the most important thing is that nothing should be allowed to restrict the offer of the gospel. Moreover, it is not just his own integrity that is at stake, but the integrity of the gospel itself. At the heart of the good news of Jesus is the grace of God: grace being the free gift of God or, as the old acronym has it, 'God's riches at Christ's expense'. Just as it has been offered freely to us, so both Paul's head and his heart compel him to pass it on just as freely.

Is laying down our rights a sign of weakness or of strength? To do so intentionally is surely a sign of strength: an indication of an inner sense of security, of trust, that enables freedom from fear or the need for self-defence. That sense of security and trust Paul has found in his encounter with the risen Jesus, transforming his 'Old Testament' understanding of God – to the extent that nothing will now stop him from sharing that new-found freedom at every opportunity.

How do we feel about our rights? What about 'human rights' in general? Is there such a thing or does this concept have more currency within the developed world, with its often strident focus on the individual? Or might one say that it is more helpful to think in terms of responsibilities: the responsibility to treat everyone with respect, with dignity, with compassion? Would the command to love our neighbour as ourselves cover it?

Gracious God, may we find such security in you that we are free to set aside any 'rights' of our own and focus on truly loving our neighbour. Amen.

SHEILA WALKER

Reading the room

For though I am free with respect to all, I have made myself a slave to all, so that I might gain all the more. To the Jews I became as a Jew, in order to gain Jews. To those under the law I became as one under the law… To the weak I became weak, so that I might gain the weak. I have become all things to all people, that I might by all means save some.

One of the key skills of a good communicator is the ability to 'read the room': that is, to see and understand the feelings, behaviour and situation of your hearers and to adapt your material accordingly. The best lesson, script or sermon will fall flat if the audience is on a totally different wavelength.

It is a mark of Paul's commitment, concern and humility that he rejects a one-size-fits-all approach to his evangelism and invests time, imagination and energy into reinterpreting his message in ways that will resonate with his hearers. He is of course a Jew and a Pharisee, but since he came to faith in Jesus Christ he no longer feels bound by Jewish laws. In his sharing of the gospel with Jews he will, however, set it within the context of Jewish history and prophecy. As to identifying with the weak, he has already written to the Corinthians that he came to them in weakness and in fear and trembling; Corinth's reputation as being cosmopolitan, rough and immoral was hardly reassuring!

It is hard to imagine Paul ever saying 'It's not my thing' or having any no-go areas. Such is his sense of urgency in sharing the new life he has been gifted that no challenge is too great to be accepted; every opportunity is too good to miss.

Of course we are not all evangelists, but we are all told to be ready to give an account of the hope we have in Jesus. Like Paul, we too have access to the Holy Spirit, to ask for the discernment to read the room, and to be given the right words for the right person.

Lord, give me the courage to ask for and to take up opportunities to share my faith in you. Amen.

SHEILA WALKER

Running to win

Do you not know that in a race the runners all compete, but only one receives the prize? Run in such a way that you may win it. Athletes exercise self-control in all things; they do it to receive a perishable wreath, but we an imperishable one. So I do not run aimlessly, nor do I box as though beating the air, but I punish my body and enslave it, so that after proclaiming to others I myself should not be disqualified.

Corinth was the venue for the Isthmian games, held every two years, so the sight of athletes training would be a familiar one for Paul's hearers. He sees a need to challenge the complacency of the Corinthian Christians, who apparently fail to realise that a moment of salvation is not the end of the story. That salvation needs now to be worked out, albeit in the power of the Holy Spirit at work in and through them. Jesus is hugely encouraging to his disciples, but he also speaks of taking up our cross, of persecution, of labouring in harvest fields. His disciples need to be fit, committed, disciplined; and there are no shortcuts to fitness.

The analogy of the race is useful, but breaks down at the point of having only one winner. Unlike in athletics, every committed Christian is a winner. We cannot be disqualified, to use Paul's words. We cannot lose our salvation. It is true, though, that our work will be tested by fire, to establish its quality: its motive, its empowering, its execution. Has it been carried out for God's glory or ours? Has it been in our own strength or through the wisdom and enabling of the Holy Spirit? This will determine the rewards we will receive, a subject on which scripture is somewhat enigmatic.

The relationship between effort and grace, between our work and God's gift, presents an ongoing challenge. It is not that our bodies will always be a source of temptation, but we recognise that body, mind and spirit can all come under attack in ways which will potentially undermine our service to God and to one another.

Lord, help me to know what kind of discipline I may need in order to serve you better. Amen.

SHEILA WALKER

Failing to please

I do not want you to be ignorant, brothers and sisters, that our ancestors were all under the cloud, and all passed through the sea, and all were baptised into Moses in the cloud and in the sea, and all ate the same spiritual food, and all drank the same spiritual drink. For they drank from the spiritual rock that followed them, and the rock was Christ. Nevertheless, God was not pleased with most of them, and they were struck down in the wilderness.

Sometimes people query whether the God of the Old Testament is the same being as the God of the New, but Paul is anxious here to point out that God's unfailing love and provision are utterly consistent. Equally predictable, though, is the presumption and faithlessness of his people, despite all his care for them. Whether long ago in the time of Moses or right up to date here in Corinth, God's people are guilty of complacency and a casual, if not arrogant, response to his many blessings.

The people of Israel were led by God's cloud in the wilderness, but fail to accept his guidance in their daily living. They eat the miraculous food and drink, but fail to take in the word of God. They are happy to benefit from God's grace, but fail to accept the implications or responsibilities of their salvation, whether through Moses or through Christ.

There is a parallel here, too, between the Israelites' baptism, or commitment, to Moses, followed by a regular provision of food and drink, and our baptism into Christ, followed by our regular 're-membering' of him as we share bread and wine.

Human nature does not change very much, if at all. There is always the danger that familiarity will breed, if not contempt, at least the tendency to take for granted the grace of God which should constantly inspire our thankfulness, awe, obedience and worship. Maybe this is also true of our other relationships: grumbling and criticism can so easily replace gratitude as our default mode, and is one of the sins that prevented the majority of the people of Israel from entering the promised land.

Lord, please show me where I can express gratitude
and appreciation this week. Amen.

SHEILA WALKER

Passing the test

So if you think you are standing, watch out that you do not fall. No testing has overtaken you that is not common to everyone. God is faithful, and he will not let you be tested beyond your strength, but with the testing he will also provide the way out so that you may be able to endure it.

There is a fine line between trusting in the grace of God and presuming on it; hence Paul's warning to the Corinthians. The fact is, we have a spiritual enemy who is never off duty, so if we are to stand and to withstand that enemy, there is a need daily to arm ourselves, as Paul underlines in his letter to the Ephesians, with the whole armour of God.

Testing may come from a variety of sources: from other people, our circumstances, our own weaknesses or failings, our spiritual enemy – even from God. When we think, like the Corinthians did, that we are doing well, then the test may be from the temptation of arrogance or self-satisfaction. If the test concerns something we feel is way beyond our capabilities, then it may be to challenge the depth of our trust in God, that he is not only able but willing to provide me – yes, even me – with all that I need to meet it. The way out, the exodus, significantly also describes the redemptive death of Jesus, the ultimate way out of all that would separate us from God. (See readings for 22–28 March.)

How often, I wonder, have we said to God: 'I know you said you wouldn't let me be tested beyond my strength, but this time you've really gone too far – I just can't cope!' I certainly have. And to challenge the text of verse 13, that is exactly what God does seem to do from time to time – testing us beyond our own strength, expressly to grow our faith as we prove his sufficiency. Despite my misgivings and indignation, I am here to tell the tale. God is faithful, if not always in the ways we expect.

Corrie ten Boom, who survived a Nazi concentration camp, said that the older she grew, the less she understood God but the more she trusted him. Lord, let it be so for me. Amen.

SHEILA WALKER

Refusing to compromise

Therefore, my beloved, flee from the worship of idols… What do I imply then? That food sacrificed to idols is anything or that an idol is anything? No, I imply that what they sacrifice, they sacrifice to demons and not to God. I do not want you to be partners with demons. You cannot drink the cup of the Lord and the cup of demons. You cannot partake of the table of the Lord and the table of demons.

In such a diverse city as Corinth, it is not surprising that all kinds of worship took place: there were major temples to Aphrodite, the goddess of love, and to Apollo, god of music, poetry and the epitome of male beauty. To challenge such a prevailing culture takes wisdom and courage, and Paul seeks both to warn and encourage the Christians in their life and witness.

While it is true that there is no significance in the actual material objects of worship, it is also true that there is a spiritual reality behind every act of worship and every participant, knowingly or not, is engaging with that reality. Paul makes a black-and-white distinction here: worship of anything or anyone other than the God of Jesus Christ is worship of something or someone seeking to take the place of the true God, and therefore tantamount to worship of the demonic.

He relates this specifically to the sharing of bread and wine at the Lord's supper, to which he will return again in the next chapter. It is a serious matter to be casual in one's approach: saying yes to Jesus means saying no to any rival allegiance.

Before we too succumb to that temptation to complacency, it is worth asking what, for us, may constitute 'idols': money, family, career, reputation, comfort? Our enemy does not usually sign his name, but assumes many disguises. In all that we do, it is helpful to ask ourselves whether we are honouring God, and perhaps whether there may be anything more he is asking of us. Idleness, as well as idolatry, may be a temptation.

Lord, please show me if there are ways in which I am compromising, and help me truly to love you with all my heart, soul, mind and strength. Amen.

SHEILA WALKER

Using freedom wisely

'All things are permitted', but not all things are beneficial. 'All things are permitted', but not all things build up. Do not seek your own advantage but that of the other. Eat whatever is sold in the meat market without raising any question on the ground of conscience… But if someone says to you, 'This has been offered in sacrifice', then do not eat it, out of consideration for the one who informed you and for the sake of conscience – I mean the other's conscience… So, whether you eat or drink, or whatever you do, do everything for the glory of God.

'All things are permitted' sounds like one of those slogans that can easily be misused. It doubtless resonated with the Corinthian Christians who were anxious to defend their liberal practices. It is true that Christians are no longer under the law and, as far as eating and drinking are concerned, the earth is the Lord's and all that is in it, according to Psalm 24:1. No longer is anything, of itself, unclean. We are free to take advantage of all that is on offer in the market or supermarket.

However, Paul is sensitive to the fact that there are likely to be some whose conscience may be more tender, albeit unnecessarily scrupulous. Annoying though it may be to limit our freedom for their sake, it is a mark of true Christian love that we will not insist on our own way, but allow for others' reservations if their faith would be shaken. Paul will return to this exploration of Christian love in the famous passage in 1 Corinthians 13. Meanwhile, he is content to remind his readers that it's not about their rights, but about building up the Christian community, the body of Christ.

Unlike the Corinthians, it may be that more often we fail to grasp the extent of our freedom in Christ – that there is absolutely nothing we need to do to earn God's love and forgiveness, it is all by grace. No demands, but also no rights.

Lord, in the face of such generosity, help me to be sensitive and generous in turn to those whose faith may be fragile. Amen.

SHEILA WALKER

Following tradition

Give no offence to Jews or to Greeks or to the church of God, just as I try to please everyone in everything I do, not seeking my own advantage but that of many, so that they may be saved. Be imitators of me, as I am of Christ. I commend you because you remember me in everything and maintain the traditions just as I handed them on to you.

I wonder how many of us would dare to echo Paul's advice to the Corinthians to imitate him, as he seeks to imitate Christ? If we feel this smacks of pride, perhaps we should also remember his willingness to forgo his rights for the sake of encouraging others to come to faith. If he points first to himself here, it is so that they may find in him a stepping-stone to encountering and imitating Christ himself. Nevertheless, it is a bold invitation!

Finally, Paul has found something for which to commend his readers: they have both heard and are committed to passing on his teaching. This in a culture where oral tradition is the prime method of communication. The traditions Paul refers to are the essential truths of the gospel and the practice of the Lord's supper, which are being passed on by the apostles and teachers to new believers and which come to constitute the foundations of apostolic faith, to this day.

The use of the word 'traditions' may well provoke mixed reactions: do they amount to peer pressure from the dead, or a recognition of the wisdom and experience of our ancestors? As in so many contexts, the challenge is to seek the Holy Spirit's discernment in our approach to tradition: not to accept it for its own sake, but to consider its depth and truth. According to the composer Gustav Mahler, tradition is not the worship of ashes but the preservation of fire – or it should be! Faithfulness to traditional teaching will not prevent us from interpreting traditions of worship for our own time and culture. Winston Churchill said that without tradition, art is a flock of sheep without a shepherd; without innovation, it is a corpse. Is this also true of our faith?

Lord, may we both appreciate and pass on good traditions, and be open to your leading into new ways. Amen.

SHEILA WALKER

Covering mysteries

But I want you to understand that Christ is the head of every man, and the man is the head of the woman, and God is the head of Christ. Any man who prays or prophesies with something on his head shames his head, but any woman who prays or prophesies with her head unveiled shames her head – it is one and the same thing as having her head shaved.

Welcome to the minefield which is any discussion of the question of gender submission! Even to unravel the cultural issues of first-century Corinth is challenging. Certainly it was normal for a woman to cover her hair: uncovered hair was the mark of a prostitute, a high-class mistress or a slave, whose head would be shaved. To remove her veil, according to Paul, would therefore dishonour not only herself but also her 'head' in the sense of her husband.

In Jewish worship the men would pray with their heads covered, but now in Christ they are set free from such laws, and should therefore demonstrate that new-found freedom, otherwise they will dishonour their 'head', meaning Christ. Previously women would have worshipped separately, hence there was no risk of flowing hair proving a distraction to the men. But in the early church, with men and women now worshipping together, this is also a practical precaution!

The Greek word for 'head' is *kephale*, which usually has the sense of source or origin. As part of the Trinity, Christ has always existed, but Paul writes to the Colossians that Christ, the Word, is also the one through, or by whom, all things were created. It would seem, therefore, that Paul asserts a creation order of God, Christ, man, woman, each to some degree deriving their identity, their glory, from their predecessors.

Do we then infer a willing submission of woman to man, just as man submits to Christ? This has been the interpretation for much of church history, though many now consider that other scriptures speak differently, as we will see tomorrow. Whatever one's view, no interpretation of male headship can ever justify male violence against women, in any form.

Father God, secure in the knowledge that you value us all equally, may we be free to lay down our right to have the last word. Amen.

SHEILA WALKER

Needing each other

Nevertheless, in the Lord woman is not independent of man or man independent of woman. For just as woman came from man, so man comes through woman, but all things come from God... But if anyone is disposed to be contentious – we have no such custom, nor do the churches of God.

You don't have to be a card-carrying feminist to want to accuse Paul of a degree of misogyny after yesterday's reading, but here he hastens to redress the balance. In no way are men to lord it over women, but to realise that we are all equally dependent on one another. Adam realised very early on that he needed Eve, that complementary helper, and God was evidently of the same view. In Christ, there is no longer male and female, as Paul wrote to the Galatians (3:28), for all are equally valued and valuable.

Conversations about gender continue to challenge and to seek to push every boundary. Whereas in Genesis 1:27 we see that God created us male and female, the situation has become more complex and fluid in terms of how people choose to self-identify. While there is a very small minority for whom gender is physically ambiguous and hugely challenging, in principle most of us fully embrace God's male/female creation order. With understanding and respect, we should encourage one another to become the people God created us to be, as perfectly as possible, as the Holy Spirit works in and through us.

It is interesting that Paul is then led to warn against a contentious, argumentative spirit, which should have no place in church circles. This is not to say that we should not be able to voice genuine differences and seek the Spirit's wisdom to bring resolution. Rather it is not allowing our time and energy to be sidetracked into unproductive wrangling which distracts us from our true priorities of service and witness.

Lord, there are times when you call us to be countercultural;
help us then to have the courage of our convictions and to share them with sensitivity and grace. Amen.

SHEILA WALKER

Fragmenting fellowship

Now in the following instructions I do not commend you, because when you come together it is not for the better but for the worse. For, to begin with, when you come together as a church, I hear that there are divisions among you… When you come together, it is not really to eat the Lord's supper. For when the time comes to eat, each of you proceeds to eat your own supper, and one goes hungry and another becomes drunk.

Unity is key. The longest prayer we know of that Jesus prayed, recorded in John 17, is for the unity of his followers. It is where there is unity that God can pour out his blessing. Why is this so?

It all relates to the fact that we, the Christian community in any one place, are to be the body of Christ: his hands and feet, his heart, his voice, his wisdom, his love. If there are divisions among us, it is as if we are a body without hearing, without sight, without mobility, with our hands tied and our feet attempting to go in opposite directions – neither attractive nor effective. We all know how incapacitating even the pain of a toothache – maybe the equivalent of just one dissenting voice – can be; how much worse when there is a significant autoimmune breakdown.

Paul makes the connection here with the Lord's supper. When we receive the bread and wine, it is both an individual and a corporate act. It is individual, in that what happens there between us and the Lord is personal; each of us may understand it somewhat differently, and the way in which our relationship with God is fed will always remain, to some extent, a mystery. But it is also a corporate act: the fact that we are sharing the same life-giving elements is making us one of a kind, one 'body'.

The Corinthians evidently had not grasped this, and Paul does not mince his words.

Lord, this is indeed something of a mystery: while we may not fully understand, help us to be truly one in you, a healthy body ready to love and serve. Amen.

SHEILA WALKER

Discerning the Lord

Whoever, therefore, eats the bread or drinks the cup of the Lord in an unworthy manner will be answerable for the body and blood of the Lord. Examine yourselves, and only then eat of the bread and drink of the cup. For all who eat and drink without discerning the body, eat and drink judgement against themselves.

Sharing bread and wine as a regular Christian practice or discipline will always move into mystery. What exactly happens will depend on the relationship between each individual and the risen Christ. Whatever our understanding, it is a sacrament: a visible, tangible sign of something which is spiritually significant but which may defy our efforts to articulate it.

Here, it is nothing less than the death of Jesus which we are called to 'remember' – that is, not just to recall the facts but in some way to enter the reality of his death and all that it accomplished for us. It therefore brings us to the very heart of our faith and challenges our response. It is a serious matter.

How, then, to ensure that we will not be unworthy of this sharing? It is certainly not that we have to be especially good before we come; on the contrary, we need to know that we are never able to shine brightly enough without the power of the Holy Spirit. The bread and wine are the food we need to persevere in our journey towards Christlikeness. It is the self-examination that matters, the refusal to allow familiarity to breed contempt, to be casual, unthinking, on automatic pilot. This was a challenge for the Corinthians, and it is for us. It is fine to celebrate in a more or less formal style, provided we approach our Lord with reverence, humility and expectation – the one who was, and who is, and who is to come.

Lord, thank you for giving us a simple, down-to-earth way in which to remember you, renew our faith and resource us for our journey. Help us to be fully present to you, and to one another, as we come, and to receive all that is being offered through the medium of bread and wine. Amen.

SHEILA WALKER

Psalms 79—89

In my hot-headed youth, I decided that the psalms were boring. Along with many people, I liked the pastoral themes of Psalm 23. I also favoured selected passages from other psalms because of the beauty of the poetry. On the other hand, the practice of including the psalms as part of weekly, and even daily, worship felt too limited, too (dread word) 'traditional' for me, a view substantiated when I first heard a church congregation trying (and failing) to chant them.

Then life happened. I grew up, got a job, got a family, read the news, thought more deeply about all kinds of issues and came to realise the huge importance of the psalms as part of scripture. While I had always liked the praise and poetry, I began to appreciate the darker side of the psalms. I read the cries of rage, the groans of despair, the frustrated yearning – and discovered that the whole of human experience is found in these ancient songs.

That's hugely significant because it means that, no matter our emotional, mental or physical state, we will probably find our feelings mirrored in words set down well over 2,000 years ago. It means that our own anger and despair, frustration and yearning, does not separate us from God. Like those long-gone poets, we can speak to God as bluntly and clearly as we choose, without fear of heavenly thunderbolts. As those long-ago poets did (although the timescale may be longer than we would like), we walk through the dark and back into the light of God's love, forgiveness and faithfulness.

In the next two weeks, we will share a section of the book of Psalms together. We shall come across some familiar phrases whose original context may be unfamiliar. We will encounter the psalmists' profound anguish at the state of their nation and the loss of their homeland. Sometimes this anguish will be hard to hear, but woven through, like a thread of gold, we will find reminders that the Lord God is good, all the time.

NAOMI STARKEY

Crying for mercy

O God, the nations have come into your inheritance; they have defiled your holy temple; they have laid Jerusalem in ruins. They have given the bodies of your servants to the birds of the air for food, the flesh of your faithful to the wild animals of the earth… We have become a taunt to our neighbours, mocked and derided by those around us. How long, O Lord? Will you be angry forever? Will your jealous wrath burn like fire? Pour out your anger on the nations that do not know you, and on the kingdoms that do not call on your name. For they have devoured Jacob and laid waste his habitation.

The scene is graphic: the psalmist sees a horde of strangers trampling the remains of the beloved city. Bodies lie desecrated on the ground, pecked by carrion birds, gnawed by wild beasts. Worst of all, the house of the Lord, the 'holy temple', has been 'defiled' and rendered unusable by ruin and degradation. Echoing in the air are the mocking laughter and cruel taunts of the conquerors.

The backdrop is the exile of God's people, the trauma of defeat at the hands of their enemies followed by a forced exit from home. They lost their inheritance – the land promised to Abraham, Isaac and Jacob (whose name is used here as another way of referring to the nation as a whole). The beloved country – hard-won through escape from Egypt, wilderness wanderings, military conquest – has been snatched away from them.

The psalmist begs the Lord to heed the cries of grief, to recognise that the broken bodies are 'your servants… your faithful'. The Old Testament prophets and chroniclers exposed the extent of the nation's wilful rebellion – but now the righteous have been punished alongside the guilty. Why should they pay such a harsh price, while those who care nothing at all for Israel's God can swagger across the sacred sites?

The calls for God to 'pour out your anger' on other nations may make us feel uncomfortable, but the longing for vengeance is, surely, understandable.

Reflect on how we handle the age-old question of why bad things happen to good people. In a national cataclysm, innocent people can be caught up in suffering that is not remotely of their making.

NAOMI STARKEY

The heavenly farmer

You brought a vine out of Egypt; you drove out the nations and planted it. You cleared the ground for it; it took deep root and filled the land. The mountains were covered with its shade, the mighty cedars with its branches; it sent out its branches to the sea, and its shoots to the River. Why then have you broken down its walls, so that all who pass along the way pluck its fruit? The boar from the forest ravages it, and all that move in the field feed on it. Turn again, O God of hosts; look down from heaven, and see; have regard for this vine, the stock that your right hand planted.

The psalmist addresses the Lord God, telling a tale of amazing agricultural achievement. The Lord was not only a farmer but one whose vine, carefully tended, grew so vigorously that it 'filled the land', from the great river Euphrates to the Mediterranean Sea. It grows until it literally puts in the shade not only mighty cedar trees but even the mountains. The farmer's hard work – clearing the ground (clearing the country) – has been rewarded.

Then comes the turning point – 'Why then…?' Why has this farmer destroyed his own handiwork, allowing passers-by to gobble the fruit and wild animals to root up that plant of such prodigious growth? The psalmist cannot understand how such tender care has turned to such cruel indifference.

While this psalm, as yesterday's, emerges from the context of exile, the emotions speak across the centuries to present-day situations where a worshipping community has broken down (or been torn apart) by human failure. The failures may be undeniable – but that does not make the pain any easier to bear. Asking God to 'restore the vineyard', to bring back the lost fruitfulness and beauty, may provide a language of prayer that eventually leads to a glimmer of hope.

Reflect on how the concept of God 'driving out the nations' requires careful unpacking and thought. We should not heedlessly affirm 'This is the word of the Lord' in response, but hold that story of conquest together with the final vision in Revelation of all the nations flocking into the new Jerusalem to worship the Lamb.

NAOMI STARKEY

No, you listen to me!

I hear a voice I had not known… 'In distress you called, and I rescued you; I answered you in the secret place of thunder; I tested you at the waters of Meribah. Hear, O my people, while I admonish you; O Israel, if you would but listen to me! There shall be no strange god among you; you shall not bow down to a foreign god. I am the Lord your God, who brought you up out of the land of Egypt. Open your mouth wide and I will fill it… I would feed you with the finest of the wheat, and with honey from the rock I would satisfy you.'

After two days of the poet calling on God to respond, here we have the opposite: 'a voice I had not known'. God speaks and, although the voice is unfamiliar, the words speak a lament that reverberates through the scriptures: 'Oh my people, why have you forgotten me? Why do you not heed me?' It is the lament of the spurned spouse or the rejected parent, where love has been given freely and received happily but then rebuffed.

The story of deliverance is rehearsed once again – the times of tumult and testing, the times of mysterious revelation ('the secret place of thunder') – and the tale of covenant is retold. We also hear the pain of the lover – or parent – who longs to give with boundless generosity but faces rejection. The offer is not mere basic rations but delicious bread and honey. There is no need to gather or bake but just open the mouth, like a baby bird, and be fed to fullness.

Relationships cannot be unrequited and still thrive. God calls his people to remember their story but also their covenant commitment to faithfulness, and to renew that covenant for the coming years. They cannot complain that the Lord has abandoned them when, in truth, it is they who walked away.

Reflect on how God's voice might be one we 'had not known'. Perhaps we can only imagine God speaking in booming operatic tones, like an old-fashioned Hollywood hero. Remember how the prophet Elijah heard the Lord in 'a sound of sheer silence' (1 Kings 19:12). What might that sound like?

NAOMI STARKEY

Challenging the powers

God has taken his place in the divine council; in the midst of the gods he holds judgement: 'How long will you judge unjustly and show partiality to the wicked? Give justice to the weak and the orphan; maintain the right of the lowly and the destitute. Rescue the weak and the needy; deliver them from the hand of the wicked.' They have neither knowledge nor understanding, they walk around in darkness; all the foundations of the earth are shaken. I say, 'You are gods, children of the Most High, all of you; nevertheless, you shall die like mortals, and fall like any prince.' Rise up, O God, judge the earth; for all the nations belong to you!

This psalm begins with the startling image of a council, with God taking his place among a number of other divine beings. We find something similar in Psalm 89 and also Job 2, where Satan (Hebrew for 'Accuser') turns up to challenge the Lord about the 'blameless and upright' Job (v. 3). Here, as there, scripture makes clear that the God of Israel is supremely powerful – 'All the nations belong to you!'

Interestingly, the Lord's judgement of the 'divine council' is not initially about their lack of true agency (although that is the verdict in the final lines). It is about how they use what power they have. These so-called gods should operate differently, behave better, than mortals – and they do not. Even if their presence somehow shakes the 'foundations of the earth', they fail to be truly god-like. They cannot lift themselves above the human obsession with status and wealth nor commit to caring for the poor and voiceless, the marginalised and dispossessed. That, says God, is true power.

If such caring lies at the heart of who our God is, it should also lie at the heart of our church communities. All too easily, social concern can end up as an 'added extra' rather than core to who we are and what we believe. Whether or not the 'voice' of our church is strong in its local context, we must ensure it speaks up for fainter voices in the community, the country and the world.

Who or what are the 'gods' that our society worships?

NAOMI STARKEY

The enemy we know

O God, do not keep silent; do not hold your peace or be still, O God! Even now your enemies are in tumult; those who hate you have raised their heads. They lay crafty plans against your people; they consult together against those you protect. They say, 'Come, let us wipe them out as a nation; let the name of Israel be remembered no more.' They conspire with one accord; against you they make a covenant – the tents of Edom and the Ishmaelites, Moab and the Hagrites, Gebal and Ammon and Amalek, Philistia with the inhabitants of Tyre; Assyria also has joined them; they are the strong arm of the children of Lot.

The land promised to God's people was a strategically significant territory for the surrounding superpowers as well as being regularly eyed-up by nearby smaller kingdoms, many of whom were actually distant relatives. While we do not need to memorise the ins and outs of Israelite family dynasties, it is noteworthy that Edom was another name for Esau (Jacob's brother), the Ishmaelites were descendants of Abraham's son (born to Hagar), and Lot was Abraham's nephew. The Assyrians were outsiders but still associated with ancient clan rivalries and disagreements.

Hatred can be so much more bitter when the enemy is known to us, hence the particular pain of civil war. Left unresolved, squabbles over resources, boundary disputes or petty personal grudges can fester and eventually turn into devastating conflict. And, says the psalmist, in fighting against God's people, the attackers become God's enemies too. Just as God made a covenant with the patriarchs, so these enemies have made their own covenant, one of evil intent.

These verses remind us that we too are allowed to be specific in our prayers. We may rightly hesitate to think of 'God being on our side', but in conflict situations, we can go ahead and name the people and forces ranged against us. That will help us connect our praying with our true feelings, rather than escaping into generalised 'godly thoughts'.

Pray that governments, communities and individuals continue to call out the prejudices that, unchallenged, are the seeds of murderous onslaught.

NAOMI STARKEY

Cry 'havoc'

Do to them as you did to Midian, as to Sisera and Jabin at the Wadi Kishon, who were destroyed at En-dor, who became dung for the ground. Make their nobles like Oreb and Zeeb, all their princes like Zebah and Zalmunna, who said, 'Let us take the pastures of God for our own possession.' O my God, make them like whirling dust, like chaff before the wind. As fire consumes the forest, as the flame sets the mountains ablaze, so pursue them with your tempest and terrify them with your hurricane. Fill their faces with shame, so that they may seek your name, O Lord.

Here the psalmist takes imprecatory prayer to a new level as various blood-curdling episodes from the book of Judges are cited to prompt God to 'act now as then'. The best-known fate is that of Sisera, army commander for a Canaanite king, who came to a grisly end thanks to a skilfully wielded tent peg.

Invoking the era of the judges meant harking back to one of the most unstable and violent eras in Israelite history. The chronicle of that time ends with the chilling verse: 'In those days there was no king in Israel; all the people did what was right in their own eyes' (Judges 21:25). Here the psalmist calls on the Lord to unleash that anarchy once again. The swirling emotion is powerfully evoked in the allusion to a forest fire, burning out of control across the mountains, stoked by hurricane-force winds. According to this petitioner, no sanctuary is granted to God's enemies.

Almost as an afterthought, there follows a demand for personal humiliation for them, in the expectation that then, and only then, will they acknowledge that true power lies with the Lord Almighty. Here is prayer of a range and level of rage that is breathtaking in its honesty but also frightening in its intensity. Dare we ever speak to God like this?

Call to mind a situation (or person) which provokes feelings of upset, even anger. Setting aside assumptions about 'what we ought to pray', ask yourself what you really feel – and what you would really like to happen. Tell God, exactly as you feel it. Then wait for God's answer.

NAOMI STARKEY

Sweetest of homes

How lovely is your dwelling place, O Lord of hosts! My soul longs, indeed it faints for the courts of the Lord... Even the sparrow finds a home, and the swallow a nest for herself, where she may lay her young, at your altars, O Lord of hosts... Happy are those whose strength is in you, in whose heart are the highways to Zion. As they go through the valley of Baca they make it a place of springs; the early rain also covers it with pools... For a day in your courts is better than a thousand elsewhere. I would rather be a doorkeeper in the house of my God than live in the tents of wickedness.

After the dark emotion of recent readings, it is a relief to arrive at these well-known and joyful verses. This is one of the 'pilgrim psalms', sung by those travelling to Jerusalem to worship at the temple. Their relief at reaching journey's end is expressed in praise for God's 'dwelling place' and delight at the numbers who makes their way there – probably on foot – over hills and through valleys, along 'the highways to Zion'.

The scene is brought to vivid life in the lovely detail of the little birds, sparrows and swallows flying to and fro and finding nesting-places amid the magnificent buildings. The house of God is a haven for every living thing, from the humblest of creatures to the grandest of kings.

As well as relating to long-ago pilgrims, this psalm has spoken to anyone passing through life's 'dark valley'. Baca has been identified as the name of a dried-up valley near Jerusalem, a place of trees oozing a kind of resin, a symbol of ongoing grief; it has also been translated as 'vale of tears'. Whatever the original reference, the underlying promise holds true of God's provision in times of pain. However bleak the outlook, the Lord's purposes are always for blessing, healing and restoration.

Although we affirm that 'the church is the people, not the building', reflect on the love that many feel for their local place of worship. It may be their 'thin place', where God's presence is sensed most clearly, even if they don't regularly attend services.

NAOMI STARKEY

Longing for the storm to pass

Lord, you were favourable to your land; you restored the fortunes of Jacob. You forgave the iniquity of your people… Restore us again, O God of our salvation, and put away your indignation towards us. Will you be angry with us forever? Will you prolong your anger to all generations?… Let me hear what God the Lord will speak, for he will speak peace to his people… Surely his salvation is at hand for those who fear him, that his glory may dwell in our land. Steadfast love and faithfulness will meet; righteousness and peace will kiss each other… The Lord will give what is good, and our land will yield its increase.

Here is intercession of the highest eloquence, begging the Lord to restore land and people to their former positions of favour. God is reminded of past blessings and mercies, before the retelling of history changes to passionate pleading for mercy. Yes, there was iniquity – but it was forgiven. Yes, there was sin – but it was pardoned. Why, then, is the storm of divine anger not abating? Has love been swept away entirely and always?

Then the psalmist's faith surges up and overflows: even if salvation is not yet here, it is 'surely at hand', because that is what the Lord is like. There has been forgiveness, favour and restoration before and there will be again, so long as the people continue to wait, hope and pray. They need God's blessing not only for themselves but for the land as well, so that it will 'yield its increase'.

In this dream of restoration, we find the beautiful image of 'righteousness and peace' exchanging a kiss. Just as love and faithfulness must bond together to build enduring relationships, so peace will be secured through conscious commitment to 'righteousness'. Modern ears may hear that as 'self-righteous' but it simply means 'choosing what's right, according to God's ways', 'walking by the light of truth and goodness'. And that is a truly secure foundation for peace-building.

If your church is in a time of flourishing, give thanks to the Lord.
If it is enduring a time of fallowness, pray to the Lord for forgiveness, renewed favour and restoration.

NAOMI STARKEY

The prayer of the poor servant

Incline your ear, O Lord, and answer me, for I am poor and needy. Preserve my life, for I am devoted to you; save your servant who trusts in you… Teach me your way, O Lord, that I may walk in your truth; give me an undivided heart to revere your name. I give thanks to you, O Lord my God, with my whole heart, and I will glorify your name forever… O God, the insolent rise up against me; a band of ruffians seeks my life, and they do not set you before them. But you, O Lord, are a God merciful and gracious, slow to anger and abounding in steadfast love and faithfulness.

The opening words of this psalm remind us of the tax collector's prayer in Jesus' parable: 'God, be merciful to me, a sinner!' (Luke 18:13). Here speaks one who trusts that they can cling to God's loving kindness; they have nothing else to offer besides honesty and commitment to right living. Even so, they beg to learn more of God's ways, to be shown the path of truth, to be given 'an undivided heart'.

Today's 24/7 culture demands multitasking and – some argue – discourages focusing on one thing at a time. On gadgets we 'doom scroll' through world news, disappear down 'rabbit holes' of endless information, and end up overwhelmed by choice. Praying for an 'undivided heart', finding our centre point in worshipping the Lord God before all else, is more important than ever.

Like the psalmist, we have the challenge of living out our faith in an indifferent, at times hostile, world. We may not have to deal with 'bands of ruffians', but 'walking in the truth' will take some effort if nobody else seems bothered. Thankfully, the simple act of prayer connects us with God's 'abounding faithfulness' and also changes us, reminding us of the heavenly perspective and eternal context for our daily lives.

Reflect on the fact that however feeble our prayers feel, however fragile our faith, we can call on our heavenly Father. We can come, just as we are, and ask for help. We can remember, too, that the Holy Spirit intercedes for us 'with groanings too deep for words' (Romans 8:26).

NAOMI STARKEY

City of joy

On the holy mount stands the city he founded; the Lord loves the gates of Zion more than all the dwellings of Jacob. Glorious things are spoken of you, O city of God. Among those who know me I mention Rahab and Babylon; Philistia too, and Tyre, with Cush – 'This one was born there,' they say. And of Zion it shall be said, 'This one and that one were born in it,' for the Most High himself will establish it. The Lord records, as he registers the peoples, 'This one was born there.' Singers and dancers alike say, 'All my springs are in you.'

This is another joyful psalm, the inspiration for the hymn 'Glorious things of thee are spoken'. Zion was another term for Jerusalem, from the name of one of the hills where David established a stronghold. Here, as elsewhere, we are called to reflect on what Zion/Jerusalem symbolises, rather than the bricks and mortar of a literal city.

The original city of David grew into the splendid capital of Solomon, home of the temple, the dwelling place of God. Although that was destroyed, this psalm affirms the hope of renewal. Israel's former enemies ('Rahab' either referring to Egypt or to a mythical monster of chaos) have become an admiring throng, watching the Lord registering the returning people of Zion. Among them are those with the strongest bond of belonging, who have actually been born there. Their delight spills over into singing and dancing, a celebration of homecoming underway even before the legal work is completed.

The promise of wrongs righted, land restored and the world renewed recurs throughout scripture, finally articulated in John the Evangelist's Revelation. Although we cannot say precisely how that promise will be fulfilled, we can be sure it will involve welcome to our Father's house and a seat at the heavenly banqueting table.

Reflect on the following: 'I saw the holy city, the new Jerusalem, coming down out of heaven from God… I saw no temple in the city, for its temple is the Lord God the Almighty and the Lamb… Its gates will never be shut by day – and there will be no night there. People will bring into it the glory and the honour of the nations' (Revelation 21:2a, 22, 25–26).

NAOMI STARKEY

The darkest place

Is your steadfast love declared in the grave or your faithfulness in Abaddon? Are your wonders known in the darkness or your saving help in the land of forgetfulness? But I, O Lord, cry out to you; in the morning my prayer comes before you. O Lord, why do you cast me off?... Wretched and close to death from my youth up, I suffer your terrors, I am desperate. Your wrath has swept over me; your dread assaults destroy me. They surround me like a flood all day long; from all sides they close in on me. You have caused friend and neighbour to shun me; my companions are in darkness.

This psalm is not for the faint-hearted – or at least not if the faint-hearted are looking for consolation. It has been described as the bleakest psalm in the Bible because there is no sudden uplift, no moment of 'But you, O Lord...' contrasting with the earlier mood of grief or anger. The cries of help remain unanswered; the final verse closes with the word 'darkness'.

The Old Testament for the most part does not speak of life after death. The grave meant 'the land of forgetfulness', also called Sheol or, as above, Abaddon, literally 'ruin'. Rather than anticipating rest with the Lord when earthly days were done, the Hebrew poets begged for God's mercy to keep them in the land of the living. Here the lamentations describe both the fear of non-existence and the struggle to survive a tsunami of suffering. The psalmist feels as if the creator is deliberately unmaking creation, allowing the original chaos to return and sweep them away, unluckiest of mortals.

They stare, unflinching, into the dark as Job was forced to do, after losing his health, wealth and family. And, like Job, they continue to seek God's presence even as they cry in despair – 'Why do you cast me off?' They battle the raging waters and cling, as to a battered life raft, to the knowledge that with the Lord there is steadfast love and faithfulness, even if hidden by the storm clouds for now.

How often do we think about our own death? How does that make us feel – and how can we pray about such feelings?

NAOMI STARKEY

Let all the world in every corner sing

I will sing of your steadfast love, O Lord, forever… your faithfulness is as firm as the heavens. You said, 'I have made a covenant with my chosen one; I have sworn to my servant David: "I will establish your descendants forever, and build your throne for all generations."' Let the heavens praise your wonders, O Lord, your faithfulness in the assembly of the holy ones. For who in the skies can be compared to the Lord? Who among the heavenly beings is like the Lord, a God feared in the council of the holy ones, great and awesome above all that are around him?

After the darkness of yesterday's psalm, we are back to the light with a psalm that soars skywards in praise. As the rising sun gilds the mountains, so God's love banishes every shadow until the universe resounds with rejoicing. We're reminded of the ancient idea of the 'council of the holy ones' (see 28 January), with the triumphant assertion that the Lord is more 'great and awesome' than any other heavenly being. God's presence with God's people means stability, security and a pledge of enduring commitment to those in his keeping.

We will spend three days with this long psalm, which centres on the theme of covenant, the bond made between God and God's chosen ones. From the very beginning, covenant is what God makes – with creation, with humanity, with Abraham and his descendants. Sadly, from the very beginning (as the Bible tells), covenant is what humanity breaks.

Then, astonishingly and because of God's steadfast love, humanity is forgiven. Ruins are rebuilt and wounds healed – but then the pattern of fall and restoration repeats. Finally, as the creeds of the church remind us, God takes human form and comes into the world. Through Jesus' death and resurrection, a new and eternal covenant is forged, opening the way to the Father's presence for everyone, forever.

'This is my blood of the covenant, which is poured out for many for the forgiveness of sins' (Matthew 26:28). The next time you 'drink the cup', try dwelling on that word 'covenant' and give thanks for God's faithfulness and forgiveness throughout the generations of human history.

NAOMI STARKEY

How long is forever?

Then you spoke in a vision to your faithful one and said, 'I have set the crown on one who is mighty; I have exalted one chosen from the people. I have found my servant David; with my holy oil I have anointed him; my hand shall always remain with him… He shall cry to me, 'You are my Father, my God, and the Rock of my salvation!' I will make him the firstborn, the highest of the kings of the earth. Forever I will keep my steadfast love for him, and my covenant with him will stand firm. I will establish his line forever and his throne as long as the heavens endure.

The promises in these verses are awe-inspiring: an eternal commitment by the eternal God. The 'line' of this 'highest of the kings of the earth' will never fail and God's protecting presence will always be around him. With that level of security established, what could this dynasty do but walk in step with the Lord?

We know, however, what actually happened to David's line, even by the time of his grandsons: the kingdom quarrelled and divided, with each part choosing a path that eventually led to exile and ruin. Yet human faithlessness does not negate the faithfulness of God. The pattern of scripture – and the pattern of life – so often involves God working through the mess and muddle, the trauma and tragedy, to bring about God's good purposes.

Our sense of 'forever' is inevitably biased towards our personal lifespan, maybe extending to a couple of generations on either side. The time beyond that lies outside our full comprehension because we were not there (and will not be there) to experience it. Hope is found, then, in trusting in the God who is 'the Alpha and the Omega… who is and who was and who is to come, the Almighty' (Revelation 1:8).

Reflect on and praise God for: 'But this I call to mind, and therefore I have hope: The steadfast love of the Lord never ceases, his mercies never come to an end; they are new every morning; great is your faithfulness. "The Lord is my portion," says my soul, "therefore I will hope in him"' (Lamentations 3:21–24).

NAOMI STARKEY

Looking for the love

But now you have spurned and rejected him; you are full of wrath against your anointed. You have renounced the covenant with your servant; you have defiled his crown in the dust. You have broken through all his walls; you have laid his strongholds in ruins. All who pass by plunder him; he has become the scorn of his neighbours... How long, O Lord? Will you hide yourself forever? How long will your wrath burn like fire? Remember how short my time is – for what vanity you have created all mortals!... Lord, where is your steadfast love of old, which by your faithfulness you swore to David?

Covenant and mortality come together in this final extract from Psalm 89. After the lines of praise comes the fatal 'But': but you, Lord, have abandoned your own covenant; but you, Lord, have destroyed your own servant; but you, Lord, have hidden from us – and we fear that you will stay hidden until our pathetically limited days are done.

As before, the psalmist expresses fears for God's reputation: why reduce your 'anointed' to an object of scorn? What will the neighbouring nations think? Instead of God's 'faithfulness' being praised 'in the assembly of the holy ones' (v. 5), serving the Lord will be viewed as – at best – a fruitless commitment, at worse a prelude to rejection and ruin. 'Forever' now means the fear of divine anger burning forever, not the hope of unshakeable and steadfast love.

Psalm 89 concludes the third of the five books into which Psalms is divided. The final verse ('Blessed be the Lord forever. Amen and Amen') acts as a coda to the 'book' as a whole rather than a last word on this psalm, which finishes on a note of beseeching. Mercy has been demanded but not yet granted; the waiting for relief is not yet over. The time for gritted teeth and plodding onwards, step by painful step, continues.

At times, life's upheavals can leave us hanging on to faith by a thread. Can we find encouragement in the psalmist's determination not to let go of God – like Jacob (Genesis 32:26) – until blessing is received?

NAOMI STARKEY

Ephesians 3—4

No letter in the New Testament matches Ephesians in integrating the cosmic scope of what God has done in Christ with its practical outworking in the daily life of the community.

At the time of writing this, I am living in an angry and anxious community. The reasons for this are unimportant; far more important is knowing how to act in a community when human dynamics become destructive. I say 'community' rather than 'church' because the lessons of Ephesians apply to any body where unity is prized.

Christ's life and death, breaking down the dividing wall of hostility between different ethnicities, groups and factions, is the pattern to achieve reconciliation in every age. And the good news is that we are not left to our own devices to follow Christ's example; rather, we are taken by the Spirit into his life – 'rooted and grounded in love'. The grace that we are given remakes us into those with hearts big enough for reconciliation.

In practice this means being able to deal with anger when others anger us, and we them. It means not only avoiding evil but actively doing good, having compassionate regard for others, acknowledging their needs and seeking to meet them. Only in this way can we model the servanthood of Jesus.

At the crucifixion, Jesus was called to suffer the converging, destructive perspectives of many groups and factions and to hold them together in his body without resorting to violence or hate. We hope and dare to pray that our hearts will be made tender enough to share in this work of non-retaliation and relationship-building, so that our suffering can be fruitful for others.

The 'Paul' who claims authorship of this letter – whether Paul of Tarsus or, as many scholars believe, a later disciple taking his mantle – makes it clear that his own suffering for the gospel is a privilege. He thought of it as a gift, enabling others to witness a reconciling life, and as a grace, bearing fruit in the lives of others.

May we respond gracefully to God's calling to live out Christ's ministry of reconciliation. Each of us is called to a unique ministry, but all of us have been made members of Christ's one reconciling body.

ROLAND RIEM

Imprisoned for the gospel

This is the reason that I, Paul, am a prisoner for Christ Jesus for the sake of you gentiles, for surely you have already heard of the commission of God's grace that was given me for you and how the mystery was made known to me by revelation, as I wrote above in a few words, a reading of which will enable you to perceive my understanding of the mystery of Christ.

Paul is not someone full of himself, though for the sake of his readers, he has to present himself winningly. Experience teaches us that the credibility of any message is inevitably bound up with the credibility of the person delivering it. If the messenger's character and credentials do not stack up, why listen to what is being said? Paul reminds the church that he is in prison for their sake. This emphasis on imprisonment is what is different from a parallel passage in the letter to the Colossians, in which Paul describes himself as a 'servant of the gospel'.

Being a prisoner for Christ can be taken both literally and metaphorically. Paul is indeed in prison, but he is also 'imprisoned' by the claim of Christ's gospel on his life, and by his costly responsibilities as Christ's apostle. There is no Plan B for him. He is totally committed to God's cause and to the well-being of the Ephesians.

Paul, though imprisoned, is under no constraint; he has been commissioned by grace and commissioned to convey grace. The overflowing, gracious favour of God runs freely through Paul to others. All is gift when it comes to his message, a mystery offering Gentiles the chance to be brought into Christ's body, as he has already written about: 'through him both of us have access in one Spirit to the Father' (Ephesians 2:18).

There is no hidden catch. The mystery is given as it has been revealed – by grace – and Paul strains to offer it to the church as best his powers on parchment permit. While he is in prison, his ministry must be channelled through what he writes, much to the benefit of future generations.

Heavenly Father, make us people not full of ourselves but filled instead by the mystery of Christ's reconciling love. Amen.

ROLAND RIEM

In God's good time

In former generations this mystery was not made known to humankind, as it has now been revealed to his holy apostles and prophets by the Spirit: that is, the gentiles have become fellow heirs, members of the same body, and sharers in the promise in Christ Jesus through the gospel. Of this gospel I have become a servant according to the gift of God's grace that was given me by the working of his power.

The work of remaking God's people took time. We, with our short attention spans and desire for quick fixes, may wonder why. It may help to compare this radical refashioning with how hard ecological change is proving. To upend our reliance on polluting fuels seems vital to our individual and national well-being, but it needs a revolution and the reforming of ways which till now we believed brought progress to humanity.

It the same with salvation: it was tied into a system involving law, national and racial identity, the temple and the land. All those things were good and bore God's promise, but unfortunately the regime as a whole created a dividing wall of hostility, alienating the Gentiles from the right to belong to God's people on equal terms. It took the revolution of the blood of Christ – Christ's whole life and death given sacrificially – to demolish this wall. And this took place in God's good time.

We might bother less about the time it took and wonder more about God's sweeping plan playing out across the generations, and be grateful that the change, when it finally came, was so well founded on the ministry of apostles and prophets. Compared to the long pedigree of the old regime, the new Christian movement might be judged to have been built on shaky ground, but Paul points out that the solidity of God's new regime rests on Christ the cornerstone, and on the grace and power marking the ministry of his apostles.

We serve the same gospel and belong to the same apostolic witness as Paul, and in our generation we have the opportunity to provide the same sense of solidity by resting on these ancient, sure foundations.

'Of this gospel I have become a servant' (v. 7),
and by this same gospel we are bound to grace and hope.

ROLAND RIEM

Called to reconcile

Although I am the very least of all the saints, this grace was given to me to bring to the gentiles the news of the boundless riches of Christ and to make everyone see what is the plan of the mystery hidden for ages in God, who created all things, so that through the church the wisdom of God in its rich variety might now be made known to the rulers and authorities in the heavenly places.

It is a blessed thing to know what you are for. People talk enviously of those with a vocation, even if sometimes they are expected to work for less for the privilege! It is indeed a privilege to be called, but a privilege for everyone, because everyone has a part to play in living out God's boundlessly rich purposes. No one could have anticipated Paul's journey from zealous Jew to apostle to the Gentiles or that a man like him, with all the rights of a Roman citizen, should end up fulfilling his work from a prison cell.

Paul has his eyes fixed on the mystery of God in Christ, which alone gives him purpose. This vision is a revelation for humanity. Everyone is included in the reality God has opened up in Christ. All our vocations are enabled because we all live in this new ethos of reconciliation, where everything is being brought into unity under Christ. This cosmic, mystical vision of what is to come can bear all the horrors of hostility and war because it cleaves to the faith that Christ's death and resurrection have irreversibly transformed the cosmos.

Each of us is called in a particular way into Christ's reconciling work. Remember how in the pandemic we suddenly saw the value of delivery drivers, keeping us all in touch and sustaining us. All of us belong to each other and each of us has a vocation to find in this bringing-together. Paul's way of being an apostle, trying to bring together Jew and Gentile in one body in the church, was vital, but it is not a template for the saints to imitate slavishly. The key to every calling is reconciliation.

May 'the wisdom of God in its rich variety' (v. 10) equip each of us uniquely to share in Christ's work of reconciliation. Amen.

ROLAND RIEM

The fruit of sacrifice

This was in accordance with the eternal purpose that he has carried out in Christ Jesus our Lord, in whom we have access in boldness and confidence through faith in him. I pray, therefore, that you may not lose heart over my sufferings for you; they are your glory.

When we suffer, in our misery we sometimes take it out on others – the 'kicking the cat' syndrome. Our suffering blinds us to the harm we are doing them and can even give it a sense of justification. We seek relief by lashing out, venting our pent-up emotions at a convenient target. These situations, however much they involve words, are really about feelings which have not yet been worked through.

Paul suffers differently: he sees his suffering in relation to others' feelings. He anticipates the way his misfortune might cause his beloved audience to lose heart. He anticipates this discouragement and prays against it. Paul does not want his witness to be anything other than a benefit to the Ephesians. If they can see his misfortune in the right way, then it will be to them a crowning glory.

If we were fortunate to have had good parents, we may not have noticed what they suffered for us. Only looking back, do we see the sacrifices they made. My mother sold off a very precious childhood teddy to pay for my school fees. She did not make a big thing of it, but when I reflect on this now, I see how she did this willingly out of love and a sense that this was a necessary act for my sake in a time of financial hardship.

Paul doesn't want the Ephesians to see his sufferings as a cause for guilt. They are credentials of his apostolic ministry – a consequence of his boldness and confidence in the gospel. The good news is that the suffering of Christ and his followers is a sacrifice which, according to God's eternal purpose, bears fruit, if not for those suffering, then certainly for other members of the church. If others can see that Paul's suffering has purpose, that it works for their salvation, then they too might grow in boldness.

Thank you, God, for the sacrifices that Christ and others have made for my glory. Amen.

ROLAND RIEM

Rooted in love

For this reason I bow my knees before the Father, from whom every family in heaven and on earth takes its name. I pray that, according to the riches of his glory, he may grant that you may be strengthened in your inner being with power through his Spirit and that Christ may dwell in your hearts through faith, as you are being rooted and grounded in love.

The glory that comes from being in the flow of others' redemptive suffering – yesterday's passage – is a pale reflection of God's own glory. God's glory is rich, always spilling over in creative ways into his work of redemption. It is capable of strengthening us at our core. We need to believe this, especially when our inner beings feel dispirited by guilt or fear and we feel that nothing can touch the void. This is a real feeling, but it is not true. Our core is not out of bounds to God. God's Spirit can work powerfully in our desolate, guilty, private spaces. God's glory is revealed as these are overtaken by God's Spirit, and our inner being is renewed in power.

This talk of power working in us should not mislead us into thinking that God recharges our batteries before moving on to the next hopeless case, as if spinning plates to keep everyone perky. As God acts within us through his Spirit, he strengthens us by moving in with us, by Christ taking deeper lodging in our heart. You cannot separate the Spirit that God sends into our inner being from the presence of Christ dwelling in our hearts, because the Spirit is given for our salvation through the Son. The Spirit is the breath of Christ's resurrection while the benefits of Christ's resurrection flow through his Spirit.

Spirit and Son working together in us effect a marvellous transformation. We become rooted and grounded in love. The passive mood of those verbs 'rooted' and 'grounded' suggests that this is God's work, to drive down into depths beyond our known, felt footings, to become the bedrock of our lives, founding them in love. Often called *agape* love, it is the same selfless, sacrificial love that we have seen exemplified by the apostle Paul.

Come Holy Spirit! Empower and earth us in love in Christ! Amen.

ROLAND RIEM

A love beyond knowing

I pray that you may have the power to comprehend, with all the saints, what is the breadth and length and height and depth and to know the love of Christ that surpasses knowledge, so that you may be filled with all the fullness of God. Now to him who by the power at work within us is able to accomplish abundantly far more than all we can ask or imagine, to him be glory in the church and in Christ Jesus to all generations, forever and ever. Amen.

The prayer finishing here began at verse 13. Paul prayed first that the Ephesians should not lose heart, then that the power of the Spirit would strengthen them. The result would be a rooting and grounding in love, with Christ dwelling in their hearts through faith.

What might they, and we, experience of this strengthening? Three important clues follow.

The first is that if we want to grasp something vast, then our capacity for grasping must increase. A young child out shopping cannot pick up a melon with one hand, but her mother can, because her hands are bigger and stronger. Paul's prayer for the Ephesians, to have the power to comprehend Christ's love dwelling in them, shows that we cannot grasp this reality without expanding our capacity to know. It is too huge in its breadth, length, height and depth.

The second qualification is 'with all the saints'. Community is not incidental to coming to know Christ's love. We can only come to know it fully with others. If you watch a great occasion alone on TV, the experience cannot match being with others amid the shouting and cheering crowd. The 'you' for whom Paul prays strength is always plural. The fullest knowledge of the love of Christ is always embedded in community.

Thirdly, there is the love that surpasses knowledge, which we inwardly know even though it is a mystery. When it comes to God and knowing his infinite love intimately, we are all like Jacob wrestling with the angel (see Genesis 32:22–32).

God, you are beyond imagining, but your fullness fills us. Amen.

ROLAND RIEM

Living the oneness of God

I, therefore, the prisoner in the Lord, beg you to walk in a manner worthy of the calling to which you have been called, with all humility and gentleness, with patience, bearing with one another in love, making every effort to maintain the unity of the Spirit in the bond of peace: there is one body and one Spirit, just as you were called to the one hope of your calling, one Lord, one faith, one baptism, one God and Father of all, who is above all and through all and in all.

After his prayer that the Ephesians would be strengthened, Paul returns to the reason why strengthening is necessary: so that the Christians gathered in community should lead a life worthy of their calling, a life of unity. The word 'one' appears seven times in rapid succession to emphasise that the unity Paul has in mind is an expression of the whole Christian life. It is not a unity of sameness; it is a unity of solidarity, transcending the boundaries of any isolated individual or group.

Everyone in the one community living in the power of the one Spirit participates in Christ's life, through faith and baptism, and therefore is drawn into the life of God the Father. There is a simplicity to this one divine life which encompasses all our differences. This does not mean, however, that these truths do not need to be worked out in relationship with others, to actualise the gospel in the life of the one body.

It is comforting to read how Paul sees relationships working towards unity. Day by day Christians need to make every effort to be unity-makers by seeking peace at every twist and turn of living together. Humility and gentleness will prevent aggressive self-assertion. Patience – literally, 'long temper' – means continually bearing with one another in love. The power of love in the hearts of those called into the body works out in relationships, in the persistence of love played out in the body.

The one gospel has not changed. The one Spirit is given to take us into Christ's life, in which we find the strength to live together in loving forbearance and in the bonds of peace.

A worthy life is lived in the bonds of peace.

ROLAND RIEM

The descent of fullness

But each of us was given grace according to the measure of Christ's gift. Therefore it is said, 'When he ascended on high, he made captivity itself a captive; he gave gifts to his people.' (When it says, 'He ascended', what does it mean but that he had also descended into the lower parts of the earth? He who descended is the same one who ascended far above all the heavens, so that he might fill all things.)

Paul shifts now from encouraging others to work for a unity founded in Christ to thinking about the diversity of gifts making up this unity. He himself is contributing to this through the gift of his own ministry. So he moves from talking of 'you' to talking about 'us'. This is what unity looks like close up, when diverse gifts contribute to the common good.

It is Christ ascended turning on the hose and showering gifts on his church. The various gifts distributed in the life of the community come by the gift of one Lord, through one baptism. We need not be afraid that this diversity will get out of hand to bring disunity, because Christ is giving them – one hand gifting the one body.

The exposition of Psalm 68:18, used to support the argument here, is not easy. It is based on later interpretations that developed in Judaism. (The original meaning concerned the Lord's ascent to Mount Zion after delivering his people.) Paul shapes the verse to fit with his vision of Christ's resurrection and exaltation being an ascent. The descent, necessary for the giving of gifts, seems at the same time to be a descent of the ascended Christ.

Christ ascended does not just fill the heavens but the 'lower parts of the earth'; he gives himself and makes himself present through his gifts. Through these gifts, given in profusion and diversity, he fills his creation. His gifts are not parachuted from heaven; Christ bears these gifts to us in person in the descending Spirit. The giftedness of the community, when the diversity works together for unity, fills the earth with the presence of Christ and connects us with the fullness of heaven.

Christ ascended and triumphant,
fill this earth with the fullness of heaven through your gifts. Amen.

ROLAND RIEM

The gifts of ministry

He himself granted that some are apostles, prophets, evangelists, pastors and teachers to equip the saints for the work of ministry, for building up the body of Christ, until all of us come to the unity of the faith and of the knowledge of the Son of God, to maturity, to the measure of the full stature of Christ.

When we think of gifts, we often think of attributes or talents given to individuals as part of their make-up. Paul, however, is connecting gifting to different forms of ministry in the early church. It may seem, then, that if we cannot identify with one of these listed official positions, then somehow our gifts are less significant. Quite the opposite! Imagine what makes someone a good evangelist. You might think of a host of essential attributes: the ability to listen, a deep faith, compassion for people, eloquence, courage, discretion, and so on. Gifting to be an evangelist requires much more than a small package of specialised gifts.

The same thing would apply to any role or position we may hold officially or unofficially. We may at times feel overwhelmed by our responsibilities in our families and communities and at work, but God has given us abundant gifts to fulfil them. We must not think of gifts as the extras added to our natural selves; rather, our gifting is what God does to grace our natural selves and raise us up. In the Spirit, we become more us. As is often said, grace builds on nature; it does not replace it.

And likewise with calling: calling is not the churchy, bolted-on bit to the activities we ordinarily undertake and the relationships and tasks to which we are already committed. These tasks, activities and commitments are rather taken into the one call on our lives in Jesus Christ, which, we are told here, is to draw all things into the building up of Christian unity, knowledge, maturity and fullness. In and through our calling, everything we do and everyone we relate to is drawn into the life of the one body, which is Christ's.

Dear Lord, fulfil your work of grace in us. Make us whole, wholly yours, wholly disposed to building up others around us. Amen.

ROLAND RIEM

Growing into truth

We must no longer be children, tossed to and fro and blown about by every wind of doctrine by people's trickery, by their craftiness in deceitful scheming; but speaking the truth in love, we must grow up in every way into him who is the head, into Christ, from whom the whole body, joined and knit together by every ligament with which it is equipped, as each part is working properly, promotes the body's growth in building itself up in love.

To put Paul's warning positively, we are aiming for maturity and stability – not to remain as children, blown so easily off course. The focus on safeguarding in church life, and the horrendous stories behind it, have sensitised us to the damaging deceit exercised by unscrupulous and determined people. They can abuse others because they have been believed, while the vulnerable have been left unprotected.

Much useful training is available to reduce risk and prevent these crimes and their terrible consequences, but here the focus is on culture. Culture is how a community or society works in practice. It is about what is tolerated and what is not, what is valued and what is not. The vision of the members of the body working and growing together should be the defining feature of Christian culture.

Speaking the truth in love is key to the way in which we grow up into this culture. Community is easily destroyed when the gap between our words and intentions widens. Then our words carry less truth, because the truth is that we are bound to each other much more closely in Christ than we might suppose: we are 'joined and knitted together by every ligament'. We are strenuously tangled together at every level, much more than faithful couples who are 'joined at the hip'. When we speak from this truth in love, this knotted spiritual intimacy, then our words will build up the body, and we will be built up in the body by them.

Speaking in other ways may bring a sense of our own superiority over others, but this cannot make for church, because in church we are bound together in Christ, and he is the only head.

Jesus, your word is truth; help us to speak your truth in love. Amen.

ROLAND RIEM

Beyond futility

Now this I affirm and insist on in the Lord: you must no longer walk as the gentiles walk, in the futility of their minds; they are darkened in their understanding, alienated from the life of God because of their ignorance and hardness of heart. They have lost all sensitivity and have abandoned themselves to licentiousness, greedy to practise every kind of impurity. That is not the way you learned Christ!

Sometimes it helps to paint up a contrast, in this case between old life and new, even at the risk of caricature. The Gentiles stand for the way of life which must be left behind, for the reasons vividly given. Behind this solemn insistence lies the lure of falling back into old ways, of trying to live between two camps. However, it is not possible to straddle like this, hedging bets, and still to grow into the inheritance of the saints.

In a few strong words Paul argues why the old life is undesirable, principally because it is futile – pointless and useless. Mental and physical health are not in competition. We are aware more than ever now of the connection between the two and of the hidden pandemic of mental illness. According to the mental health charity Mind, in the course of a lifetime one in five people will have suicidal thoughts, one in 14 people self-harm and one in 15 people attempt suicide. Futility is a frightening, destructive prospect.

Out of dark and empty minds and from hearts cut off from the creative wellspring of life come all kinds of bitter fruit. What is left within us when our internal moorings are broken is a bundle of naked desires which seem to promise freedom if we abandon ourselves to them but which bring only death. Practising the dark arts of impurity and immorality is a sure way to learn futility.

Learning Christ, on the other hand, is the surest way to life. This means coming to know the one dwelling in our hearts through the Spirit, who ends our alienation from God and each other. All human desires can be reordered and renewed around our deep desire for him.

Without you, Lord, we are but dust and ashes;
with you our dust is reborn. Amen.

ROLAND RIEM

New clothing for a new self

For surely you have heard about him and were taught in him, as truth is in Jesus, to put away your former way of life, your old self, corrupt and deluded by its lusts, and to be renewed in the spirit of your minds, and to clothe yourselves with the new self, created according to the likeness of God in true righteousness and holiness.

The passage here amplifies what has just been said about the contrast between the former and the renewing ways. There are some important words and phrases which accent these different directions away from and towards discipleship. On the negative side, we can be deluded by our lusts. The consistent perspective of this letter to the Ephesians is that our passions can rule and overtake us. We might think we can use our passions to achieve drive and fulfilment, but tragically passions indulged corrupt and delude us. They are not tame and acquiescent energies; unchecked and undisciplined, they can choke and pollute the streams of life within us.

We must put away this former way of life without Christ in order to put on the new self. Perhaps the unclothing and reclothing imagery relates to the rites of the early church, where candidates were stripped for baptism, then reclothed as they emerged from the baptismal waters. Rather than looking to lust to animate us, we can be drawn instead more fully into 'truth as in Jesus'. This phrase carries so much weight. There are many lessons to learn about Jesus but in the end the lesson is Jesus, because truth dwells in Jesus.

As we clothe ourselves with the new self, this living Jesus-truth pervades the mind. His presence affects the 'how' of our thinking, the 'spirit of our minds', as well as the 'what' of our thinking, the subjects perennially at play in our heads. True righteousness and holiness can never be a matter of externals. What is envisaged here is a complete renewal of God's image in us: as God is totally and indivisibly holy and righteous, we cannot, as we are renewed in Christ, desire anything less than to reflect that complete integrity.

'Reclothe us in our rightful mind, in purer lives our service find' (John Greenleaf Whittier, 1807–92).

ROLAND RIEM

Being truthful

So then, putting away falsehood, let each of you speak the truth with your neighbour, for we are members of one another. Be angry but do not sin; do not let the sun go down on your anger, and do not make room for the devil. Those who steal must give up stealing; rather, let them labour, doing good work with their own hands, so as to have something to share with the needy.

The change from a life alienated from God to a life renewed in Christ and lodged in his body has basic ethical consequences. The truth that each member of the body shares inwardly in Christ must work out outwardly in truthful relationships with neighbours. Neighbours – those who interact with us – have the right to truth. Without it, relationships run aground and collaboration becomes impossible. In truth-telling we create trust and grow intimacy, whether inside or outside the church, which is essential for the well-being of the whole body of society.

The relationship between anger and truth-telling is subtle. The journalist Ambrose Bierce is reputed to have said, 'Speak when you are angry and you will make the best speech you will ever regret.' We smile in recognition of the danger of speaking out of our own righteous indignation and wounds. We feel that being angry allows us to set empathy for our neighbours aside, to speak our own truth irrespective of theirs. But if we hold on to anger and let it simmer, the devil can make sport with us, and we soon find ourselves rehearsing nastiness and plotting hurt. It is wise advice that we should not sleep on our anger but try to resolve our relationships, with truth and gentleness, before sundown.

Truth and honesty go hand in hand. It is not enough simply to avoid being dishonest. A thief who stops thieving is not being dishonest, but a thief who starts using his hands differently to do honest work, feeding not only himself but others in need, has begun to act out of the truth of Christ. Christ used his hands to feed the hungry and heal the sick, and that is the life to which we must commit ourselves in his body.

Help us, Lord Jesus, to live out your truth daily in practice. Amen.

ROLAND RIEM

Tenderising the heart

Let no evil talk come out of your mouths but only what is good for building up, as there is need, so that your words may give grace to those who hear. And do not grieve the Holy Spirit of God, with which you were marked with a seal for the day of redemption. Put away from you all bitterness and wrath and anger and wrangling and slander, together with all malice. Be kind to one another, tenderhearted, forgiving one another, as God in Christ has forgiven you.

The practical advice about how to live in Christ continues. It is reassuringly simple but brings together reality and resolve. The reality is that a new body has been created by the reconciling death of Jesus. Nothing can change that, but how will this come into effect? This depends on the moment-by-moment resolve of members of the body, in this case what they do with their mouths. Just as Paul made a contrast between stealing and working for those in need, here the contrast is between something completely destructive and wrong in itself – evil talk – and something which realises the reconciliation won by Christ.

Some see the other negatives mentioned here – bitterness, wrath, anger, wrangling and slander – as a picture of the way in which anger is felt and then festers, until it explodes into petty strife and bad-mouthing others. At the very least it is a list of different facets of anger that prevent the well-being of the body.

Once again it is quite clear that the positive behaviour encouraged, as the negative is put away, is the imitation of Christ, with forgiveness being its crown. Being kind and tender-hearted is easy towards those who are kind to us. Being kind and tender-hearted to those who have upset and offended us entails being forgiving and not allowing anger and bitterness a foothold.

While human resolve is vital in overcoming the trials of community life, none of these struggles happen without God. The Holy Spirit makes his presence felt in us. We know what it is like to feel the Spirit's grief in our hearts when we trip up; likewise, we know the feeling of delving into the peace and joy of redemption.

'Batter my heart, three-person'd God' (John Donne, 1572–1631).

ROLAND RIEM

Zechariah

To us, Zechariah's prophecy can feel as if it is buried in the Old Testament, in an unfamiliar world. In terms of the timing, he whose name means 'Yahweh remembers' wrote around about 520–518 BC, two months after Haggai's prophecy. Admittedly, Zechariah's visions include scenes that we might find difficult to interpret with their various symbols, images and pictures. At the heart, however, his message is simple but profound, the loving invitation from God to his people to return to him.

In this book, God desires that the Israelites would reclaim their place physically in Jerusalem, if they have not already returned after their exile to Babylon, and to rebuild the temple, which lay in ruins. God also seeks for them to return to him emotionally, that they would once again be bonded in love to their God. The message of this book therefore also applies to us today, with God always wanting us to come home to him.

There being 14 chapters in Zechariah, it seemed appropriate to work through parts of each chapter in succession. If you have time, I encourage you to read the full chapter for more context. We will see in the first eight chapters the task before the people of rebuilding the temple, with this physical act symbolising a return in their hearts to God. The final six chapters then address the Israelites after they have rebuilt the temple. Here Zechariah offers God's judgement for their wrongdoing, but he also passes along the promise of the coming Messiah – he who will set into motion their complete restoration.

Today marks the first full week of Lent, and it feels an appropriate time to be delving into the words of this Old Testament prophet, with Lent being a time when many people examine their hearts and minds and seek to return to God if needed. As we reach the end of this ancient prophecy, we will be able to appreciate the words not only applied to God's people at the time, but how Jesus fulfils God's promise of the one who will save.

I pray that you will be enriched during our explorations with these challenging but encouraging words of God.

AMY BOUCHER PYE

Return to God

The word of the Lord came to the prophet Zechariah son of Berekiah, the son of Iddo: 'The Lord was very angry with your ancestors. Therefore tell the people: this is what the Lord Almighty says: "Return to me," declares the Lord Almighty, "and I will return to you," says the Lord Almighty. Do not be like your ancestors… They would not listen or pay attention to me, declares the Lord… Then they repented and said, "The Lord Almighty has done to us what our ways and practices deserve, just as he determined to do."'

'Oh, I don't like reading the Old Testament,' a friend said to me. 'It's just so… hard.' What I found surprising about her admission was who it came from – a person who writes and speaks about the Bible. Although I could understand her sentiments, I found myself expressing my love for the books in what is also known as the Hebrew Bible. It can feel difficult at times, but undergirding the narrative is God's love for his people.

We see this here in the opening chapter of Zechariah. The Lord calls his people back to himself, inviting them to return, to live in communion with him again. Part of that return involves rebuilding the temple, which had crumbled into ruins for decades. His invitation is therefore physical in nature – for them to continue the work of rebuilding his house after their return from captivity. But God's deep passion is more that his people themselves would return to him with their hearts and their actions – that they would turn from their 'evil ways' and 'evil practices' (v. 4), even though their ancestors did not.

On this first Sunday of Lent, God extends to us similarly an invitation to return to him, which he couples with his promise to return to us. During this season of examining our hearts and minds, I hope and pray that we will receive God's 'kind and comforting words' (v. 13) and his 'mercy' (v. 16).

God of the old and the new, help me to examine my motives and my actions through your Spirit, that I might be cleansed and renewed. Amen.

AMY BOUCHER PYE

A wall of glory

Then I looked up, and there before me was a man with a measuring line in his hand. I asked, 'Where are you going?' He answered me, 'To measure Jerusalem, to find out how wide and how long it is.' While the angel who was speaking to me was leaving, another angel came to meet him and said to him: 'Run, tell that young man, "Jerusalem will be a city without walls because of the great number of people and animals in it. And I myself will be a wall of fire around it," declares the Lord, "and I will be its glory within."'

Zechariah experienced a series of night visions, of which this is the third. The visions come from God and are a means of God seeking his people's restoration, even as they repent and return. Here the Lord uses the imagery of walls to convey his relational intent, that he himself will surround his people fully, including even their animals. Jerusalem will again be a place of safety and security as God provides his protection through a wall of fire. No marauding enemies will be able to penetrate his defences.

The prophet's use of this language of fire as related to God would bring to the original audience's mind how God brought their ancestors out of Egypt through a pillar of fire at night (see Exodus 13:21–22) or how God's glory appeared as 'a consuming fire on top of the mountain' when Moses spoke with him (see Exodus 24:17). God wants to continue his story of redemption and promise; he will not abandon his people. As Zechariah said, the Lord 'will again choose Jerusalem' (v. 12). They only needed to 'shout and be glad' (v. 10), and to 'be still before the Lord' (v. 13).

For us today, a fruitful practice can be to visualise in prayer God encircling us – our loved ones, our homes, our communities – as a ring of fire. What might you ask God to encircle today?

Circle me, Lord; keep evil out and goodness within. Circle me, Lord; keep anxious thoughts out and peace within. Circle me, Lord; keep bitterness and rage out and love and mercy within. Amen.

AMY BOUCHER PYE

Clothes of righteousness

Then he showed me Joshua the high priest standing before the angel of the Lord, and Satan standing at his right side to accuse him... Now Joshua was dressed in filthy clothes as he stood before the angel. The angel said to those who were standing before him, 'Take off his filthy clothes.' Then he said to Joshua, 'See, I have taken away your sin, and I will put fine garments on you'... 'This is what the Lord Almighty says: "If you will walk in obedience to me and keep my requirements, then you will govern my house and have charge of my courts, and I will give you a place among these standing here... In that day each of you will invite your neighbour to sit under your vine and fig-tree," declares the Lord Almighty.'

We enter, in this next vision given to Zechariah, a courtroom scene involving God, Joshua (a high priest of God's people) and his accuser. As with the other priests – those mediating God's words and grace to his people – Joshua had been physically away from Jerusalem, the holy city, during the exile. But now the Lord assembles the opposition along with Joshua to reinstate the priestly duties on his chosen one, as symbolised through the removal of the filthy garments and the donning of clean clothes.

We might quickly jump from this story of Joshua, whose name means 'God delivers', to the gift of God through his son Jesus, through whom we are promised the cleansing of our sin. We are not wrong to see promises of deliverance, but we also benefit from looking at the original context. After all, for those who had returned, and especially those who still languished in exile, the promise of restoration and renewal would have brought real encouragement. That God would 'remove the sin of this land in a single day' (v. 9) would have restored for them hope for the future.

We might consider prayerfully what rags we wish for God to remove as he replaces them with his fine robes.

Loving God, thank you that I am not left to fester in the rags of sinfulness, but that you cleanse me and restore me to my place at your table. Amen.

AMY BOUCHER PYE

Restoration

Then the angel… woke me up, like someone awakened from sleep. He asked me, 'What do you see?' I answered, 'I see a solid gold lampstand with a bowl at the top and seven lamps on it, with seven channels to the lamps. Also there are two olive trees by it'… So he said to me, 'This is the word of the Lord to Zerubbabel: "Not by might nor by power, but by my Spirit," says the Lord Almighty'… Then the word of the Lord came to me: 'The hands of Zerubbabel have laid the foundation of this temple; his hands will also complete it. Then you will know that the Lord Almighty has sent me to you. Who dares despise the day of small things…?'

We move to a vision filled with symbols and images, including lamps, golden pipes, olive trees and capstones. Many commentators have debated this vision's meaning and application and concluded that the main point is the power and restoration of prophecy. For instance, they see the lampstand signifying the rebuilding of the temple and the lamps as God's eyes and therefore God's presence in the earth.

Among this, what stands out to me are two of the statements, which today we may bandy about in Christian circles: 'Not by might nor by power, but by my Spirit' and 'Who dares despise the day of small things?' As applied in this original context, we understand how God wants his people to believe that he will restore them to their status as his people, with all the rights and responsibilities that entails. But this restoration will come through his Spirit and not through means of power or might. Thus they should not disparage the small things, for God is sovereign.

God restores his people; God will rebuild the temple. Today we can receive the grace of God through the indwelling Spirit, which he poured out following Jesus' death and resurrection. We act as God's temple here on earth, an astounding act of grace. As we ponder this gift, may we trust that we share his goodness and grace with those we meet.

God of restoration, help me to follow you and bear your presence in a hurting, yearning world. Amen.

AMY BOUCHER PYE

Laws for living

I looked again, and there before me was a flying scroll. He asked me, 'What do you see?' I answered, 'I see a flying scroll, twenty cubits long and ten cubits wide.' And he said to me, 'This is the curse that is going out over the whole land; for according to what it says on one side, every thief will be banished, and according to what it says on the other, everyone who swears falsely will be banished. The Lord Almighty declares, "I will send it out, and it will enter the house of the thief and the house of anyone who swears falsely by my name. It will remain in that house and destroy it completely, both its timbers and its stones."'

The next vision that Zechariah experiences comes with heaviness, as it includes the punishment for wrongdoing. The flying scroll, which probably would have been stretched out in Zechariah's imagination, could symbolise the ten commandments, especially with its detailing of the eighth and ninth commandments, not to steal or lie. God was emphasising the importance of the law, which he gave his people so that they would flourish. When he gave the law, he limited their freedoms only because he knew what could befall them if they went astray. As they indeed had experienced during the exile, when they were forced out of their beloved city of Jerusalem.

We might bristle at the thought of God pronouncing a punishment or his requirement that we follow his law, especially as we live in a modern-day society that places so much emphasis on the rights of the individual. But God knows what we need, and the law stands even with the coming of his Son. As Jesus said, 'Do not think that I have come to abolish the Law or the Prophets; I have not come to abolish them but to fulfil them' (Matthew 5:17).

Many Christian communities read aloud from the ten commandments during Lent. Perhaps today you could ponder these rules for flourishing, and as you do so notice which ones capture your attention.

God of justice and God of mercy, thank you that you love perfectly. Shower me with your goodness this day, I pray. Amen.

AMY BOUCHER PYE

God's presence with us

I looked up again, and there before me were four chariots coming out from between two mountains – mountains of bronze... The angel answered me, 'These are the four spirits of heaven, going out from standing in the presence of the Lord of the whole world'... And he said, 'Go throughout the earth!' So they went throughout the earth... The word of the Lord came to me... 'Take the silver and gold and make a crown, and set it on the head of the high priest, Joshua son of Jozadak. Tell him this is what the Lord Almighty says: "Here is the man whose name is the Branch, and he will branch out from his place and build the temple of the Lord."'

The appearance of the four horses gives a sense of completeness to the cycle of night visions, namely because the horses appear in the first vision (see Zechariah 1:8–11). Here the animals symbolise the Spirit of God eager to move throughout the earth and to subdue the nations. The horses, however, await the command of the Lord before they take off.

Zechariah then moves from the heavenly visions to what is happening there among the exiles. God wants his people to rebuild the temple; he desires to live among them again and to show them his faithfulness. His repeating of calling forth Joshua as his chosen one signals the authority he places on him. Not only does he want to spread his presence throughout the earth – the four horses released in the world – but he wants to dwell with his beloved ones in the house they build for him. He wants them to yearn to be with him, even as he longs for them.

As it is Lent, and we often focus on the sacrifice of the one who is God and human, perhaps you might want to consider prayerfully the great high priest, he who is 'clothed with majesty' (v. 13), who left his home in heaven to become embodied, to live, to die and to rise again. How does this age-old story speak to you in the light of this passage from Zechariah?

Gracious Lord Jesus, thank you for your love and sacrifice.
May your Holy Spirit rest within me today. Amen.

AMY BOUCHER PYE

True religion

'Should I mourn and fast in the fifth month, as I have done for so many years?' Then the word of the Lord Almighty came to me: 'Ask all the people of the land and the priests, "When you fasted and mourned in the fifth and seventh months for the past seventy years, was it really for me that you fasted? And when you were eating and drinking, were you not just feasting for yourselves?"'... And the word of the Lord came again to Zechariah: 'This is what the Lord Almighty said: "Administer true justice; show mercy and compassion to one another. Do not oppress the widow or the fatherless, the foreigner or the poor. Do not plot evil against each other."'

Our next episode comes two years after Zechariah's night visions, when the people ask God about their practice of fasting. From our vantage point, we might find God's answer surprising. After all, the people's question seems to centre on how they can honour God. The Lord, however, sees through to the heart. He points out their mixed motives during the time of exile, when they focused more on their own cravings instead of putting God first.

God desires their devotion, and that they would treat each other well. He wants them to care for those less well off; those who are far from home or who lack a familial safety net. Even as he shows them mercy and compassion, so he wants them to embrace these attributes in their interactions with those in need.

Lent can feel like a long and lonely season, one that we may embrace with eagerness at the start but then grow weary of in the messy middle. Perhaps you might consider now how you could approach the weeks to come – with the help of the Holy Spirit – as then later you will be more equipped to withstand the rigours of these weeks. God promises to grace us with his Holy Spirit and to bring forth in us his fruit to bless others.

Faithful God, you love those living at the margin. Help me to notice and become aware of those who are faltering as you show me how to extend your love and grace. Amen.

AMY BOUCHER PYE

A place for play

The word of the Lord Almighty came to me… This is what the Lord says: 'I will return to Zion and dwell in Jerusalem. Then Jerusalem will be called the Faithful City, and the mountain of the Lord Almighty will be called the Holy Mountain.' This is what the Lord Almighty says: 'Once again men and women of ripe old age will sit in the streets of Jerusalem… The city streets will be filled with boys and girls playing there'… This is what the Lord Almighty says: 'I will save my people from the countries of the east and the west. I will bring them back to live in Jerusalem; they will be my people, and I will be faithful and righteous to them as their God.'

Zechariah shares a series of oracles – promises from God each beginning with the words 'This is what the Lord Almighty says'. After hearing some of the punishment that God would mete out in the previous chapters because of his people's disobedience, we might find these words of grace and mercy especially refreshing. Perhaps these oracles act as a bridge between God's delivering of judgement and his promises of hope.

I especially love God's picture of older people sitting together and of play in the streets of Jerusalem (vv. 4–5). He shares that these communal areas will not be overcome with fighting and strife, but will be a safe place for the most vulnerable to dwell. Children will be able to roam and laugh – what a universal, all-inclusive image this is!

As it is Sunday today, and thus a feast day during Lent, might you consider relaxing any of your fasts from this season and instead embrace feasting, laughter, play and communion? I know some people prefer to continue with their disciplines for the whole of Lent, while others embrace the 'Sunday is a feast day' outlook. Whichever way you choose, may you know the playful love of an affirming God of mercy and grace.

Loving Lord God, thank you for creating a world where we can play and relax. Help me to embrace a pattern of living that includes a healthy balance between work and resting. Amen.

AMY BOUCHER PYE

Lowly king

Rejoice greatly, Daughter Zion! Shout, Daughter Jerusalem! See, your king comes to you, righteous and victorious, lowly and riding on a donkey, on a colt, the foal of a donkey. I will take away the chariots from Ephraim and the war-horses from Jerusalem, and the battle-bow will be broken. He will proclaim peace to the nations. His rule will extend from sea to sea and from the River to the ends of the earth. As for you, because of the blood of my covenant with you, I will free your prisoners from the waterless pit. Return to your fortress, you prisoners of hope; even now I announce that I will restore twice as much to you.

We move in chapters 9—14 to Zechariah's two final oracles. He would have shared these with some of God's people who were still in exile and some whom had returned to Jerusalem. Through these words, Zechariah calls God's people back to his city while also imparting the hope that God will return to them.

This prophecy can also be applied to the coming of Jesus, the man who was God. Indeed, each of the four gospels either references or alludes to this passage when they recount the events of what we call Palm Sunday, when Jesus arrives in Jerusalem riding a donkey. They share not how he arrived in glorious triumph on a war horse as a political messiah who would crush their enemies, but as one proclaiming peace, as Zechariah foretells.

Neither the original listeners of the Old Testament book nor those for whom the gospels were written would have fully understood the fulfilment of this prophecy – that which we glimpse more fully in the Bible. We can ponder how in Jesus' second coming he will enact God's perfect plan of peace that extends 'from sea to sea' as God restores all that has been lost.

Before this glorious return, Jesus submitted to his death on the cross, which we consider during Lent. May our ponderings be enriched as we consider the promises from the Hebrew Bible of the righteous yet lowly king riding on a donkey.

Saving Jesus, thank you for being a different kind of king,
one who rules with peace and grace. Amen.

AMY BOUCHER PYE

The good shepherd

Ask the Lord for rain in the springtime; it is the Lord who sends the thunderstorms. He gives showers of rain to all people, and plants of the field to everyone. The idols speak deceitfully, diviners see visions that lie; they tell dreams that are false, they give comfort in vain. Therefore the people wander like sheep oppressed for lack of a shepherd. 'My anger burns against the shepherds, and I will punish the leaders; for the Lord Almighty will care for his flock, the people of Judah, and make them like a proud horse in battle... I will strengthen Judah and save the tribes of Joseph. I will restore them because I have compassion on them.'

Zechariah's prophecy confirms that God's people suffer under poor leadership. But what is the connection between God sending the rains and then Zechariah's swift shift to addressing idolatry? Bible commentators see the connection through how God provides for his people with soaking rain, which brings forth a flourishing of crops, unlike the Egyptians who depend on the flow of water from the River Nile. But when God's people turn astray, he withholds the rain, and they experience drought. Poor leadership through false prophets and the lack of a good shepherd contribute to their hardness of heart.

Yet as we see, God promises his compassion and care; his anger will not burn forever. He assures them that he will strengthen his people and provide the security they need.

As we consider this passage, I invite you to ponder the gift of water, that which God sends through the rain and snow to nourish the earth. Each time you boil a kettle or wash your hands, you might want to call to mind the gift of living water; you could ask God to reveal to you his love through this basic part of life. You might also want to pray for leaders, not only of churches but those who lead nations and people groups, that they would be good shepherds who exercise justice, goodness and truth.

King of kings and Lord of lords, you are the good shepherd who leads me to quiet pastures. Restore my soul. Amen.

AMY BOUCHER PYE

End times

A prophecy: the word of the Lord concerning Israel. The Lord… declares: 'I am going to make Jerusalem a cup that sends all the surrounding peoples reeling… On that day, when all the nations of the earth are gathered against her, I will make Jerusalem an immovable rock for all the nations. All who try to move it will injure themselves… Then the clans of Judah will say in their hearts, "The people of Jerusalem are strong, because the Lord Almighty is their God"… And I will pour out on the house of David and the inhabitants of Jerusalem a spirit of grace and supplication. They will look on me, the one they have pierced, and they will mourn for him as one mourns for an only child, and grieve bitterly for him as one grieves for a firstborn son.'

We move to another prophecy of Zechariah, this one apocalyptic in nature. These prophecies are famously challenging to interpret. We may call to mind so-called prophets who interpret the 'signs of the times' and announce the end of the world on a particular day, only to then revise when the world does not, in fact, end. In contrast, Zechariah delivers God's words of warning to the nations without naming a particular timeframe, and how Jerusalem will be his beacon that testifies to his goodness and mercy.

Amid the hardship and upset with the nations, God promises a spirit of repentance – that of grace and supplication. We see in Zechariah's reference to one pierced the foreshadowing to Jesus on the cross, he whose side was sliced open by the Roman soldier's spear. In the ancient world, such a piercing would most often lead to death, which fits with the mourning of which Zechariah speaks.

Perhaps we could see in this apocalyptic passage the invitation to pray about strife, wars and the shedding of blood in our world. As we look to the Prince of Peace, the one whose side was pierced for our sake, we can ask him to release his grace, love and truth in a world needing his peace.

Gracious God, help me to be a peacemaker, to share your love and light.
Through your wisdom, give me an understanding of deep issues
that can divide. Amen.

AMY BOUCHER PYE

Purification process

'On that day a fountain will be opened to the house of David and the inhabitants of Jerusalem, to cleanse them from sin and impurity. On that day, I will banish the names of the idols from the land, and they will be remembered no more… Awake, sword, against my shepherd, against the man who is close to me!… Strike the shepherd, and the sheep will be scattered, and I will turn my hand against the little ones. In the whole land… two-thirds will be struck down and perish; yet one-third will be left in it. This third I will put into the fire; I will refine them like silver and test them like gold. They will call on my name and I will answer them; I will say, "They are my people," and they will say, "The Lord is our God."'

Zechariah continues with this final prophecy, one that heralds a time of winnowing, of refining as in the purification of silver or gold. We can probably imagine the great heat that is needed to remove the impurities from these precious metals, an image that Zechariah employs to warn God's people that a time of testing is coming. God will not tolerate the worship of false gods among his people. He desires total commitment, even if that entails a purification process. Afterwards he will declare to the remnant that he is their God and they are his people, his chosen ones.

We might embrace the season of Lent as a time of self-examination and the testing of our faith, to hold before God our hearts as we ask him to cleanse us from our sins. We utter this prayer believing that God will allow this process of purification, which might be painful because of the consequences of our sinful actions and thoughts, for our ultimate good. We do so trusting and believing that he does so as a loving parent, one who seeks the best for his beloved children. How might God lead you today in the confessing of sin in order that he might release you into a more pure and holy life?

Saving God, thank you for your loving process of purification.
Help me to want to be cleansed from my sins. Amen.

AMY BOUCHER PYE

Holy to the Lord

A day of the Lord is coming, Jerusalem, when... I will gather all the nations to Jerusalem to fight against it; the city will be captured, the houses ransacked... Then the Lord will go out and fight against those nations... It will be a unique day – a day known only to the Lord – with no distinction between day and night... On that day there will be one Lord, and his name the only name... On that day 'Holy to the Lord' will be inscribed on the bells of the horses, and the cooking pots in the Lord's house will be like the sacred bowls in front of the altar. Every pot in Jerusalem and Judah will be holy to the Lord Almighty... And on that day there will no longer be a Canaanite in the house of the Lord Almighty.

Our final encounter with Zechariah's prophecy continues his glimpse of the end times, the times to come. God continues his focus on Jerusalem, the holy city, heralding some of the images we see in Revelation, such as the river of life and the day that has no night. Note, too, an image unique to Zechariah about the everyday items that are made holy, the cooking pots that become sacred bowls. This reference reassures God's people that everything that is ordinary will yet be welcomed into God's kingdom of grace and light. And not only welcomed but also transformed into something that becomes a sacred vessel.

How much more are we, God's people, changed and transformed by his indwelling Spirit and made holy. This will happen fully after we die or the end times come, but God promises to continue with his purifying work each day that we live in his kingdom of heaven here on earth. Which, of course, is why we might embrace the season of Lent as a time of fasting and examination, that God would help us to live more fully as changed beings through the work of his Spirit. May you glory in these wonderful truths!

Loving God, thank you for your amazing work of grace and redemption in my life. I dedicate myself to you and to your kingdom of grace and truth. Amen.

AMY BOUCHER PYE

Jesus: for or against? Matthew 11—12

Over the next two weeks we will be looking at a section of Matthew's gospel which describes in some detail the turmoil that surrounded the ministry of Jesus. After the first year of popularity, the second year was stormier, as opposition to the coming kingdom began to grow.

Matthew 11—12 present us with several important themes. We are given a beautiful picture of Jesus as the true servant who came in fulfilment of Old Testament prophecy to bring justice and freedom. We have an opportunity to see him at work and be reminded that he still longs to set people free today.

Then there is the theme of doubt and unbelief, which may particularly resonate with some readers. Faith does not come easily to all, and even when we do believe we may find ourselves doubting. The experience of John the Baptist after he was imprisoned highlights this tension for us.

Controversy was never far away from Jesus, and his clash with the Pharisees over how to observe the sabbath emerges as a battle for the truth – a clash between mercy and compassion and the rigidity of strict adherence to man-made rules and regulations. Jesus is seen as a liberator and champion of grace over law.

Opposition to his ministry came not only from human sources, however. We read here of the grip that Satan can have on individuals and the fierce conflict between two kingdoms – the kingdom of darkness and the kingdom of light – a battle which still rages today, although it is often unseen.

Behind everything that happens, though, is the reality of the kingdom of God. Jesus has come to call men and women to live under the rule of God, to give themselves wholly to doing the Father's will. It is a challenging message and one which underlies all his teaching. It raises the ultimate question for each of us: are we for Jesus or against him?

Lent is traditionally a time for reflection. Hopefully these readings will help in that process, as each of us takes time to consider our own response to Jesus and his kingdom.

TONY HORSFALL

Are you the one?

After Jesus had finished instructing his twelve disciples, he went on from there to teach and preach in the towns of Galilee. When John, who was in prison, heard about the deeds of the Messiah, he sent his disciples to ask him, 'Are you the one who is to come, or should we expect someone else?' Jesus replied, 'Go back and report to John what you hear and see: the blind receive sight, the lame walk, those who have leprosy are cleansed, the deaf hear, the dead are raised, and the good news is proclaimed to the poor. Blessed is anyone who does not stumble on account of me.'

John the Baptist was a fearless prophet, calling people back to God and preparing the way for Jesus. He had been imprisoned because he had rebuked King Herod for his adultery and evil ways. Previously he had been certain that Jesus was the Messiah, but now, languishing in his cell, he is beset by doubts.

Doubt is not the same as unbelief. Even the strongest believers may at times find themselves wondering if their confidence in God is misplaced. Disappointment and failure, the pain of grief and loss, feelings of unworthiness or ineffectiveness can each gnaw away at our assurance. John, great man that he was, needs reassurance.

The response of Jesus is to inform John of the miraculous interventions surrounding the coming of the kingdom of God, events that clearly confirm his identity as the promised Messiah. John had not been mistaken, and his trust was not misplaced.

Did this message relieve John's distress? We cannot say, but doubt is not always easily shaken off. For John there would be no miraculous intervention, no sudden release from captivity. Sometimes we do not understand the ways of God, and hence the reminder from Jesus that, even in the darkness of doubt, we are called to trust him: 'Blessed is anyone who does not stumble on account of me' (v. 6).

Lord, I pray for those who are imprisoned for their faith today to find new strength in God, and also for any trapped in the prison of doubt and fear. Be their deliverer, Lord, even as you are mine. Amen.

TONY HORSFALL

What did you go to see?

As John's disciples were leaving, Jesus began to speak to the crowd about John: 'What did you go out into the wilderness to see? A reed swayed by the wind? If not, what did you go out to see? A man dressed in fine clothes? No, those who wear fine clothes are in kings' palaces. Then what did you go out to see? A prophet? Yes, I tell you, and more than a prophet. This is the one about whom it is written: "I will send my messenger ahead of you, who will prepare your way before you."'

John's preaching in the desert had been quite a spectacle. He was an unusual figure in appearance and way of life, and his fiery rhetoric soon drew crowds of people even to such a remote location. What at first was a novelty soon became a serious challenge, calling people to repentance and holy living. He was bold and forthright, confronting religious hypocrisy and calling for social justice. When Jesus appeared, asking for baptism, John had no hesitation in identifying him as the promised Messiah.

Now it is the turn of Jesus to bear witness to John's significance. He was the one sent by God to be his messenger, preparing the way for the Messiah (Malachi 3:1) and his message needs to be heeded, both in its moral challenge and testimony to Jesus. He is not to be regarded as a freak show or cranky revivalist. John is more than simply a prophet. He was God's messenger, and people should give attention to what he had said. He was undoubtedly a man sent from God.

It is easy to be drawn to religious gatherings as a form of spectacle – for some, the vibrancy of the worship, the eloquence of the preacher, the stimulus of being part of a large crowd; for others, the pomp and ceremony, the beauty of liturgy and choral singing, the architecture and history of the building. Yet Christian experience is not fundamentally about any of these things. It is about an encounter with a holy God who calls us to repentance and a recognition of Jesus, the long-awaited Messiah.

Lord, forgive me if I sometimes get carried away by the 'show'.
Help me to see Jesus and respond accordingly. Amen.

TONY HORSFALL

The kingdom of God

'Truly I tell you, among those born of women there has not risen anyone greater than John the Baptist; yet whoever is least in the kingdom of heaven is greater than he. From the days of John the Baptist until now, the kingdom of heaven has been subjected to violence, and violent people have been raiding it… To what can I compare this generation? They are like children sitting in the market-places and calling out to others: "We played the pipe for you, and you did not dance; we sang a dirge, and you did not mourn." For John came neither eating nor drinking, and they say, "He has a demon." The Son of Man came eating and drinking, and they say, "Here is a glutton and a drunkard, a friend of tax collectors and sinners."'

Jesus continues with his affirmation of John, the last of the prophets. His ministry marked the transition from the old covenant into the new, and with it the arrival of the kingdom of God.

The kingdom of God is the rule of God in the lives of men and women, and this is what Jesus came to establish. John was not part of this, and so, great as he was, anyone who enters the kingdom is, in a sense, greater: such is the privilege of being part of the new order.

Verse 12 highlights the opposition there is to the kingdom of God, presumably from Satan's kingdom, the Jewish religious establishment and political rulers. We see this opposition towards Jesus throughout the gospel story. We see the same antagonism as violent men like Saul seek to destroy the fledgling church (Acts 8:1–3). Even today in many parts of the world those who identify as followers of Jesus may be persecuted for their faith.

Those opposed to the rule of God can never be satisfied. John was criticised for his ascetic lifestyle, Jesus for mixing with people regarded as sinners. A society rejecting God will never welcome the kingdom of God.

Lord, opposition to your kingdom is a sobering reality in today's world. Grant courage to your people everywhere. Amen.

TONY HORSFALL

Seeing is not always believing

Then Jesus began to denounce the towns in which most of his miracles had been performed, because they did not repent. 'Woe to you, Chorazin! Woe to you, Bethsaida! For if the miracles that were performed in you had been performed in Tyre and Sidon, they would have repented long ago in sackcloth and ashes. But I tell you, it will be more bearable for Tyre and Sidon on the day of judgement than for you. And you, Capernaum, will you be lifted to the heavens? No, you will go down to Hades. For if the miracles that were performed in you had been performed in Sodom, it would have remained to this day. But I tell you that it will be more bearable for Sodom on the day of judgement than for you.'

A common assumption is that seeing is believing. We think that if something miraculous occurs, people will believe in God. But surprisingly that is not always true – those who do not want to believe always find a reason not to believe.

On a youth camp in Wales, a young man declared that if when walking through the hills that day he saw a bat, he would believe. It was a sunny day and there were few trees, but to everyone's amazement, around midday and in the most unlikely of places, there was a bat, asleep in a tree. Yet he refused to believe his own request, dismissing it as simply coincidence.

Much of the ministry of Jesus took place in Galilee, around towns like Capernaum, but the many miracles they saw did not convince people there either. They heard the teaching of Jesus, saw him at work, yet stubbornly refused to repent and believe. They did not want to live under the rule of God.

Jesus was staggered by their unbelief, given the enormous privilege they had in seeing his ministry first-hand. Even the Gentile towns of Tyre and Sidon would have believed if they had witnessed these events, and wicked Sodom would have repented at such a divine visitation. Their wilful rejection of the truth will leave them without excuse on Judgement Day.

Lord, thank you for every indication you give us of your presence. May I treasure such moments and respond with faith. Amen.

TONY HORSFALL

Childlike but not childish

At that time Jesus said, 'I praise you, Father, Lord of heaven and earth, because you have hidden these things from the wise and learned, and revealed them to little children. Yes, Father, for this is what you were pleased to do. All things have been committed to me by my Father. No one knows the Son except the Father, and no one knows the Father except the Son and those to whom the Son chooses to reveal him.'

Why is it that some people find it hard to believe? Perhaps because, as Jesus suggests here, they are unwilling to become childlike in their approach to spiritual truth. The religious leaders of the day were proud of their education and extensive knowledge of ritual customs, yet when the kingdom of God came in the person of Jesus, they could not see it and missed the moment. They were blinded by their own learning and traditions.

Spiritual truth, according to Jesus, is not simply a matter of human understanding but of revelation. If miracles will not persuade us, neither will human reasoning. We must not downplay the importance of learning but humbly recognise that intellectual pride can be a hindrance to faith. To know God, we need him to open our eyes, what the apostle Paul called 'the eyes of our heart' (Ephesians 1:17–18). He prays for the church at Ephesus to receive the Spirit of wisdom and of revelation so they can know Jesus better. A man of giant intellect himself, he knew that human reason alone was insufficient in grasping God's truth.

This means that we must become childlike in our response to God – humble enough to admit our ignorance and simple enough to trust his words. Only then will the light dawn on our souls. There is a way of knowing God. Jesus fully knows what God is like, and he will give us the insight we need.

Sadly, many adults have become cynical and sceptical. Perhaps hurt by their experience of church or organised religion, they close their hearts defensively, afraid to trust anyone again, let alone God.

Lord, help me to be more childlike in my response to you,
willing to learn new things and humble enough to ask for your help. Amen.

TONY HORSFALL

Finding rest

'Come to me, all you who are weary and burdened, and I will give you rest. Take my yoke upon you and learn from me, for I am gentle and humble in heart, and you will find rest for your souls. For my yoke is easy and my burden is light.'

Today's passage is short, and marks the end of chapter 11, but it packs a mighty punch! It contains, in my opinion, some of the greatest words that Jesus ever spoke and provides us with the key to living the life of discipleship, offering a pattern which stands in stark contrast to that taught by the Pharisees.

Jesus invites us into a partnership with himself, to be joined or 'yoked' to him. Rabbis of the day used this expression to describe the way their pupils would commit themselves to following their master's teaching and way of life. Jesus calls his followers to do the same.

Perhaps the idea of being so committed is daunting, but we need have no fear of being taken advantage of or being abused. Jesus, our teacher, is humble and gentle in the way he leads and will never exploit or harm us. He deals kindly with us. Furthermore, his yoke is easy and his burden light – he will not overwhelm us with demands and conditions or ask too much of us; indeed, he will help us to accomplish everything he asks of us.

Such an approach is so different to the legalistic religion of the Pharisees, which weighed people down with rules and regulations. Jesus invites those of us worn out with trying to live that way to find rest in him, rest for our souls. This is the good news of the gospel. We do not have to strive in our own strength to serve God. We are invited into a partnership with Jesus, where he will teach us how to work together *with* him, not simply work *for* him. There is a huge difference.

Lord, this is indeed good news! Thank you for your understanding of me. Take away my fear of giving myself fully to you. Help me to grasp that your yoke is easy, your burden is light. May I know the deep rest of which you speak. Amen.

TONY HORSFALL

Cornfield controversy

At that time Jesus went through the cornfields on the Sabbath. His disciples were hungry and began to pick some ears of corn and eat them. When the Pharisees saw this, they said to him, 'Look! Your disciples are doing what is unlawful on the Sabbath.' He answered, 'Haven't you read what David did when he and his companions were hungry? He entered the house of God, and he and his companions ate the consecrated bread – which was not lawful for them to do, but only for the priests... If you had known what these words mean, "I desire mercy, not sacrifice," you would not have condemned the innocent. For the Son of Man is Lord of the Sabbath.'

Controversy was never far away from Jesus. Here, a stroll through the fields brings him into a sharp exchange with the Pharisees, the powerful group of religious teachers ever watchful for infringements of Old Testament laws.

Much of their energy went into defining exactly what people could or could not do on the sabbath, a day of rest given to worship God when no work was permitted. They formulated over 600 different stipulations to guide people in their sabbath observance, taking the matter way beyond what God required and turning the day of rest into a burden.

Jesus was more concerned with people's well-being than the observance of humanly made regulations. Picking a few grains of corn did not constitute reaping as the Pharisees asserted. Even David put the welfare of his troops before a strict adherence to the letter of the law, allowing them to eat bread from the tabernacle rather than starve. Mercy must be at the heart of true religion and be given higher value than secondary concerns.

Jesus' radical teaching on the sabbath increasingly brought upon him the wrath of the religious elite, but his message was clear – the sabbath is intended to be a day of rest and blessing, not of burden and misery.

Lord, you have always in mind the welfare of your people. As the Son of Man, and Lord of the Sabbath, you have the right to challenge our wrong perspectives. Help me to enjoy the gift of sabbath rest and to be merciful in all I do. Amen.

TONY HORSFALL

People matter

Going on from that place, he went into their synagogue, and a man with a shrivelled hand was there. Looking for a reason to bring charges against Jesus, they asked him, 'Is it lawful to heal on the Sabbath?' He said to them, 'If any of you has a sheep and it falls into a pit on the Sabbath, will you not take hold of it and lift it out? How much more valuable is a person than a sheep! Therefore it is lawful to do good on the Sabbath.' Then he said to the man, 'Stretch out your hand.' So he stretched it out and it was completely restored, just as sound as the other. But the Pharisees went out and plotted how they might kill Jesus.

The understanding of the meaning and purpose of the sabbath continued to be a battleground as Jesus introduced the good news of the kingdom, where love and mercy have greater value than rules and regulations. He does not hide from controversy. Indeed, he seems to welcome it, because he realises that the stronghold of religious legalism must be broken if people are to enjoy life in the kingdom.

The healing of the man with a withered hand shows again that the principles of mercy and doing good triumph over any petty interpretation about what constitutes working on the sabbath. It may seem obvious to us that a person is of more value than a sheep, but scrupulously guarding the rules of sabbath observance made the Pharisees blind to the obvious work of God and lacking in compassion.

Perhaps the man's shrivelled hand is a picture of religion as presented by the Pharisees, a system void of power and ineffective. His healing demonstrates the adjustment that Jesus wants to bring, a restoration to true, life-giving faith in God.

It seems extraordinary that an act of kindness should antagonise the Pharisees to the extent that they want to kill Jesus, but religious bigotry can sadly lead people to such extremism. Jesus has touched a nerve, and the reaction is violent (remember Matthew 11:12).

Lord, I thank you for your example of kindness in healing this unnamed man. May I always walk in the way of love, showing mercy to those in need. Amen.

TONY HORSFALL

Here is my servant

Aware of this, Jesus withdrew from that place. A large crowd followed him, and he healed all who were ill. He warned them not to tell others about him. This was to fulfil what was spoken through the prophet Isaiah: 'Here is my servant whom I have chosen, the one I love, in whom I delight; I will put my Spirit on him, and he will proclaim justice to the nations. He will not quarrel or cry out; no one will hear his voice in the streets. A bruised reed he will not break, and a smouldering wick he will not snuff out, till he has brought justice through to victory. In his name the nations will put their hope.'

Matthew's purpose in writing his gospel is to help Jewish readers understand that Jesus is the long-awaited Messiah, and one of the ways Matthew makes his point is by identifying ways in which Jesus fulfilled Old Testament scriptures. Here he sees the ministry of Jesus as the fulfilment of Isaiah 42:1–4, which describes the work of the unnamed servant of the Lord. Matthew has no doubt that the person spoken about is Jesus.

As the true servant of God, Jesus came in the power of the Spirit to bring justice to all. He did not draw attention to himself or seek fame and recognition. He handled people with care and dignity, gently bringing healing and freedom to them. Ultimately, his mission will be victorious and people worldwide will put their trust in him. Such is the calling of the servant.

Jesus himself must have been aware of scriptures like this and of his call to be the servant of the Lord, but not everyone made the connection. Crowds followed him, but more for what he could do for them than who he was. They saw his power but not his person.

Lord, I recognise that you are the one of whom Isaiah spoke, the servant of the Lord. I worship you for the beauty of your character, so full of mercy and compassion, humility and justice. And I ask you to minister to me as well. Where I am bruised, heal me; when I am weary, revive me. I place myself in your gentle hands today. Amen.

TONY HORSFALL

Freedom

Then they brought him a demon-possessed man who was blind and mute, and Jesus healed him, so that he could both talk and see. All the people were astonished and said, 'Could this be the Son of David?' But when the Pharisees heard this, they said, 'It is only by Beelzebul, the prince of demons, that this fellow drives out demons.' Jesus knew their thoughts and said to them, 'Every kingdom divided against itself will be ruined, and every city or household divided against itself will not stand. If Satan drives out Satan, he is divided against himself. How then can his kingdom stand?... But if it is by the Spirit of God that I drive out demons, then the kingdom of God has come upon you.'

The powerful ministry of the servant is now demonstrated by the compassionate way Jesus brings freedom to a man who has been demon-possessed. This is the kind of victory over evil that Isaiah had spoken about (Matthew 12:20) and which demonstrates the presence of God's kingdom. Once more, however, controversy and conflict are not far away.

We are given here a glimpse into the unseen realm where Satan is at work and a reminder that his kingdom is entrenched on the earth, keeping people in darkness and robbing them of God's blessing. The arrival of the kingdom of God to bring freedom and liberty means that a spiritual battle is inevitable. This Satanic opposition is another strand of resistance that Jesus had to combat throughout his ministry.

Jesus does not operate with the assistance of demonic powers, but by the power of the Spirit, who came upon him at his baptism, as prophesied by Isaiah (Matthew 12:18). Here is a power encounter where the kingdom of God triumphs over the kingdom of Satan, a prelude to a much greater victory that Jesus would win at the cross.

Lord, as the servant you are humble, but I know you are not weak. You can set the captives free and break any stronghold, and you love to do so. We are broken people, in a broken world. Break the chains in my life, in the lives of those I know, and in the lives of all oppressed by the devil. Amen.

TONY HORSFALL

Binding the strong man

'Or again, how can anyone enter a strong man's house and carry off his possessions unless he first ties up the strong man? Then he can plunder his house. Whoever is not with me is against me, and whoever does not gather with me scatters. And so I tell you, every kind of sin and slander can be forgiven, but blasphemy against the Spirit will not be forgiven. Anyone who speaks a word against the Son of Man will be forgiven, but anyone who speaks against the Holy Spirit will not be forgiven, either in this age or in the age to come.'

Here are further insights into the nature of the spiritual battle that wages between the kingdom of Satan and the kingdom of God. What is happening in the unseen, spiritual realm occasionally spills over into the visible, everyday world. The conflict is real, and Jesus was aware of it. Although it may seem strange to contemporary western eyes and ears, in many parts of the world there is a greater familiarity with spiritual powers.

Satan is likened to a strong man who must be bound before his goods can be plundered – that is, people released from his grip. This may refer to prayer that uses God's authority to curtail Satan's activity, but more likely is an anticipation of the victory that Jesus will win over Satan at the cross. There Satan will be defeated once and for all.

In attributing the work of Jesus and the Spirit to demonic powers, the Pharisees are making a grave mistake (Matthew 12:24). Sin is only unforgiveable when people refuse to repent and seek forgiveness. If the Pharisees did repent, they could be forgiven even for such a slander. However, when they refuse to repent, hardening their hearts, they place themselves outside the realm of grace, a sad place to be.

Sensitive people may fear they have committed an unforgiveable sin, but their expression of concern is a sure sign they have not. Forgiveness is always available for those who ask.

Lord, I realise that in this clash of kingdoms there is no neutral ground. We are either for you or against you, building the kingdom or undermining it. Show me how to work with you, to help not hinder. Amen.

TONY HORSFALL

Your words betray you

'Make a tree good and its fruit will be good, or make a tree bad and its fruit will be bad, for a tree is recognised by its fruit. You brood of vipers, how can you who are evil say anything good? For the mouth speaks what the heart is full of. A good man brings good things out of the good stored up in him, and an evil man brings evil things out of the evil stored up in him. But I tell you that everyone will have to give account on the day of judgement for every empty word they have spoken. For by your words you will be acquitted, and by your words you will be condemned.'

In language reminiscent of John the Baptist, Jesus charges the Pharisees with being 'a brood of vipers', that is a nest of evil people who hang out together and stir one another up to do evil things. Strong language indeed.

Words are extremely powerful, and they do betray what is happening inside us. As Jesus says here, 'The mouth speaks what the heart is full of.' If I am absorbed with the success of the football team I support, I will often be found talking about their latest result; if I am taken up with my family, I will often be heard speaking of their most recent happenings.

More seriously, the slandering of Jesus by the Pharisees (Matthew 12:24, 32) is an indication of the evil intent of their hearts. They are set against him and want to kill him. They speak out of the jealous hatred stored up in their hearts, and they betray their wicked intentions.

If a bad tree bears bad fruit, so a good tree will produce good fruit. When our hearts are right with God our words will be healing, strengthening others and glorifying God. We will speak from the well of love and kindness within us and our words will bring encouragement and hope to others.

It is sobering to realise that our words betray what is in our hearts, and that we will give account for them.

Lord, teach me to think before I speak and choose my words carefully. Help my conversation be full of grace, seasoned with salt (Colossians 4:6). Amen.

TONY HORSFALL

An empty fish and an empty tomb

Then some of the Pharisees and teachers of the law said to him, 'Teacher, we want to see a sign from you.' He answered, 'A wicked and adulterous generation asks for a sign! But none will be given it except the sign of the prophet Jonah. For as Jonah was three days and three nights in the belly of a huge fish, so the Son of Man will be three days and three nights in the heart of the earth. The men of Nineveh will stand up at the judgement with this generation and condemn it; for they repented at the preaching of Jonah, and now something greater than Jonah is here.'

It is common for people who doubt to ask God for a sign to prove that he exists. This group of Pharisees, while perhaps not as strongly opposed to Jesus as the others, are misguided in their request. If they want a sign, there have been plenty already in the miracles that Jesus has performed. To ask for a sign now is an indication of their lack of faith.

Jesus never gave in to this form of spiritual blackmail and refused to be some kind of wonder worker desperately trying to impress and gain a following. Rather, he points his critics to two great miracles – one from the past (the sign of Jonah) and one that will happen in the future (his resurrection).

Jonah's story is a remarkable one. Thrown overboard from a ship, he was swallowed by a large fish and remained in the stomach of the creature before being vomited out alive after three days and nights. During this time, his heart was changed, and instead of running away from God he repented and went to preach to pagan Nineveh.

Jesus says Jonah's experience is a picture of his own, for he too will spend three days and nights in the tomb, a reference of his coming death and resurrection. This will be the greatest sign of all and evidence of his identity as the Son of God. If Nineveh repented because of Jonah, people should repent because of Jesus.

Lord, I know you died and rose again. You are indeed the Son of God, alive and active today, and at work in my life. Amen.

TONY HORSFALL

Part of the family

While Jesus was still talking to the crowd, his mother and brothers stood outside, wanting to speak to him. Someone told him, 'Your mother and brothers are standing outside, wanting to speak to you.' He replied to him, 'Who is my mother, and who are my brothers?' Pointing to his disciples, he said, 'Here are my mother and my brothers. For whoever does the will of my Father in heaven is my brother and sister and mother.'

The ministry of Jesus was full of ups and downs. Some people believed and accepted his message; others were vehemently opposed to him and refused to believe. His words and actions could be divisive. People were either for him or against him. Being a disciple involved a stormy ride, one moment sharing in his popularity, the next feeling the hatred towards him.

After a period of this sort of volatility, his mother and brothers arrive and we might assume that their presence will be a precursor to calmer moments, but that is not the case. Jesus undoubtedly loved his family, but there are no special privileges when it comes to kingdom living. Earthly relationships do not merit favoured treatment. The criterion for discipleship is the same for all – what matters is not who you are, but whether your aim in life is to do the will of the Father.

A willingness to obey God, no matter what, is at the heart of the kingdom, for the kingdom of God is nothing less than the rule of God in the hearts of those who voluntarily yield to his lordship. Those who do so – like the disciples gathered around him – are his family, his kin, joined to him through the common bond of loving obedience.

This is radical teaching and not easy to accept, and we might wonder if we can attain such a standard, but God knows our hearts and helps us all the way, gently coaxing us to deeper surrender. We may not be fully there yet, but what matters is the direction of our hearts – it is where we hope to be, God helping us.

Lord, I do desire to follow you fully. Help me when I fail and give me strength to go again. Amen.

TONY HORSFALL

The Passover and the second exodus

The first Passover commenced the first exodus, which gives its name to the book which describes it. Jesus shared a commemorative Passover meal with his disciples the night before his crucifixion, and therefore it is reasonable to assume that in celebrating the first Eucharist (thanksgiving), he did something at and to the Passover meal, evolving it into the liturgical meal of remembrance which so many celebrate to this day in churches and communities worldwide. Just as there would be no Christianity without Judaism to precede it, there would not be a last supper without Passover to precede it.

There would be no second exodus without the first one. 'Ex' means 'out' and 'hodos' is 'road' – an 'exodus' is a road out of somewhere or something. In Luke 9:31 Jesus speaks of the 'exodus' he will accomplish at Jerusalem. It is a little clue to the greater, second exodus: the second journey of salvation, which is described in the second, or new, Testament, which testifies to the second or 'new' covenant, which is the new relationship God forges with his people by sending Jesus to lead God's people from the wilderness of sin, death and judgement to resurrection life.

These are the themes of the Easter Vigil liturgy, which is sometimes celebrated in churches on Easter Eve, as darkness falls, or as light dawns on Easter morning. It is a profound and patient reliving of the story of salvation, from creation through to the empty tomb. In darkness the gathered people await the dawn when the risen Christ will appear. The new Passover of the Lord is welcomed with the warmth and light of a fire and candle as the familiar story is retold. The Jewish Passover continues to await a Messiah, whereas in Christianity, 'the Lord is risen': risen indeed to bring in the new creation and the second exodus.

Yet in the celebrations of both Passover and Easter there are common elements of storytelling and contextualisation, and of a celebratory meal.

As we travel through this week towards Holy Week and Easter, let us look a bit more closely at the similarities and multidirectional meanings to be found in the story of the first Passover which led to the first exodus, prefiguring the second exodus and influencing the manner of its remembrance.

GORDON GILES

The flock of God's folk

Tell the whole congregation of Israel that on the tenth of this month they are to take a lamb for each family, a lamb for each household. If a household is too small for a whole lamb, it shall join its closest neighbour in obtaining one; the lamb shall be divided in proportion to the number of people who eat of it. Your lamb shall be without blemish, a year-old male; you may take it from the sheep or from the goats.

The metrical setting of Psalm 100, known as the 'Old Hundreth', has the lines: 'We are his folk, he doth us feed, and for his sheep he doth us take.' William Kethe made the original paraphrase in 1560–61, and in some editions of the English version of the Genevan Psalter, the word 'folcke' was misprinted as 'flocke', which coincidentally connects with the reference to sheep in the following line.

In Hebrew culture, there was no distinction between a sheep and a goat. They were flocked together, and a 'lamb' could be a 'kid' – a young goat. In the parable of the judgement of the nations (Matthew 25:31–46), a shepherd separates the sheep from goats in judgement. That story tells us that God makes distinctions we do not, even if at the Passover a kid was considered equivalent to a lamb. In their young, 'innocent' state that distinction did not apply. Either is sacrificial: the 'lamb' resonates for us as 'Lamb of God', as John the Baptist called Jesus (John 1:36), and the goat as the 'scapegoat' (see Leviticus 16:15–22). In that legislation a goat is sacrificed for the people, but another one is set free to carry the sins of the people into the wilderness: a form of redemption.

The Passover celebration is fundamentally communal. The first Passover was an occasion at which families came together and included neighbours. Salvation, freedom, rescue and redemption from sin are not personal nor individual but social. There is companionship in adversity, hospitality in hopefulness: the sharing of bread and meat in hopeful expectation of a journey of rescue. Thus the folk of God form a flock as they hide and flee.

Jesus, our shepherd, may we remain always as members of your flock, under your living care. Amen.

GORDON GILES

Deflecting death

'They shall take some of the blood and put it on the two doorposts and the lintel of the houses in which they eat it. They shall eat the lamb that same night; they shall eat it roasted over the fire with unleavened bread and bitter herbs… You shall let none of it remain until the morning… This is how you shall eat it: your loins girded, your sandals on your feet, and your staff in your hand, and you shall eat it hurriedly. It is the Passover of the Lord… The blood shall be a sign for you on the houses where you live: when I see the blood, I will pass over you, and no plague shall destroy you when I strike the land of Egypt.'

As the final deadly plague descended on Pharaoh's Egypt, Moses is commanded to mark the doorposts with the blood of a lamb so that, as the angel of death passed over, the firstborn of the Israelites would not be killed. It is chilling. No wonder they ate their meal with shoes on their feet in anticipation of fleeing from Egyptian slavery. They must have been terrified. Modern equivalents might be those dissidents in Soviet Russia – the composer Dmitri Shostakovich among them – who kept a bag packed at all times in case the secret police come for them in the night. We cannot imagine the palpable fear. People are going to die tonight. Will it be me? How can I protect myself?

Moses has the answer and it is all they have – there is no alternative suggestion. They must flee, but it is better to hit the road with full bellies.

To some extent they daubed their doorposts for two reasons. Firstly, to ward off the swooping angel of death, a sign to steer them away. Yet some would have known that deflecting the angel of death would lead to anger, blame and retribution. Putting blood on the threshold would send a message to the Egyptians too: a warning, to stay away and let them go. To bereaved Egyptians the brutally bloodied doorways must have been a terrifying sight after a night of horror.

Hear our prayer for all who sleep in fear this night,
and guard all who are persecuted for their faith. Amen.

GORDON GILES

Wings of life

‘Go, select lambs for your families, and slaughter the Passover lamb. Take a bunch of hyssop, dip it in the blood that is in the basin, and touch the lintel and the two doorposts with the blood in the basin. None of you shall go outside the door of your house until morning. For the Lord will pass through to strike down the Egyptians; when he sees the blood on the lintel and on the two doorposts, the Lord will pass over that door and will not allow the destroyer to enter your houses to strike you down. You shall observe this as a perpetual ordinance for you and your children.’

Jewish communities still come together in families or groups to mark Passover. In the shared Passover meal, eating, drinking and scriptural reminders blend to create a powerful act of commitment to, as well as remembrance of, God’s deliverance. The celebration of Holy Communion is very similar in purpose and function. Every Jew at the Passover is expected to recall the first exodus as though they themselves were there, making it something of a personal as well as communal redemption. Similarly, at the Eucharist we join together in common remembrance, purpose and prayer, giving thanks for the (second) deliverance brought by Jesus.

The word ‘passover’ is not adequately translated in English: in Hebrew the verb used to refer to the angel of death’s ‘passing over’ of the blood-marked houses of the Israelites is *pasha*, from which we get the words ‘Pesach’ and ‘paschal’. It is probably derived from an ancient Egyptian word *pesh*, meaning ‘to spread wings over’. Thus Passover is not just about the avoidance of death or judgement, it also implies God’s merciful protection.

This is borne out by Jesus, who says, ‘Jerusalem… How often have I desired to gather your children together as a hen gathers her brood under her wings’ (Luke 13:34). This resonates with the true meaning of ‘passover’. It also reminds us of God the Father’s loving desire to save us, by sending his Son as paschal lamb, who in turn compares himself to a mother protecting her young with wrapped wings. Mixed as the metaphors may be, they are rich and powerful.

God, as we remember the deliverance you bring in Christ,
surround us with your loving care. Amen.

GORDON GILES

Passover Lamb of God

'When you come to the land that the Lord will give you, as he has promised, you shall keep this observance. And when your children ask you, "What does this observance mean to you?" you shall say, "It is the Passover sacrifice to the Lord, for he passed over the houses of the Israelites in Egypt when he struck down the Egyptians but spared our houses."' And the people bowed down and worshipped. The Israelites went and did just as the Lord had commanded Moses and Aaron; so they did.

After the first Passover, a *seder* (order of service) developed. This was written down in the third century AD in the Mishnah (the first written version of rabbinic law). The meal commenced with the *Kiddush*, a prayer said over the first cup of wine. Ceremonial hand-washing preceded a dish of bitter herbs (lettuce), which was dipped into salt water or vinegar. Then the second cup was poured and the youngest male would ask about the Passover's origin and in answer the story and significance of the exodus were expounded. More food was consumed, the second cup drunk and Psalms 113—114 sung.

After more hand-washing, bread was broken, blessed and dipped in the herbs and *charoseth* (a sweet mixture of fruit and nuts which symbolised the clay of Egypt) before being distributed. Only then came the lamb: the last food on the menu. The third cup of wine was poured and thanksgivings offered. Psalms 115—118 were recited, the fourth cup consumed and a closing hymn sung.

This ritual meal evolved from the first Passover and Jesus celebrated it in the upper room rather like this with his friends on the night before he died. In doing so he recast it by taking the bread and one of the cups of wine and effectively saying, 'This is me – do this [take bread and wine] in remembrance, not of the first exodus but of the second, not in memory of Moses but in remembrance of me.'

To those of us who eat and drink of the Lord's body and blood regularly and frequently, it is so easy to lose sight of not only the context of this simple act, but also its radical nature.

Jesus, Lamb of God, bless your people
as they remember you in word and sacrament. Amen.

GORDON GILES

Be gone!

At midnight the Lord struck down all the firstborn in the land of Egypt, from the firstborn of Pharaoh who sat on his throne to the firstborn of the prisoner who was in the dungeon and all the firstborn of the livestock. Pharaoh arose in the night, he and all his officials and all the Egyptians, and there was a loud cry in Egypt, for there was not a house without someone dead. Then he summoned Moses and Aaron in the night and said, 'Rise up, go away from my people, both you and the Israelites! Go, serve the Lord, as you said. Take your flocks and your herds, as you said, and be gone. And ask a blessing for me, too!'

We reflected on Monday how terrifying that night must have been. Eating a quick dinner as fuel for the journey and painting their lintels with blood was a desperate measure. It has been suggested by those who try to give a less supernatural account of what happened that the eldest child would fetch the grain from the store and that it was somehow contaminated in a deadly manner, such that those who got near to large quantities might inhale fumes and so suffocate or be poisoned. Yet neither Hebrew nor Egyptian culture had any other way of comprehending such a tragedy other than by divine intervention. They shared a fear of the divine, and now, finally, the God of the Hebrews had done something they could not ignore.

There is just enough time to get away. The Hebrews are prepared while the Egyptians are thrown into confusion. In a moment of weakness, Pharaoh, whose own heir is dead, relents. He asks for a blessing on himself, which inspires pity; but it is not long before despair gave way to counterattack. He changes his mind as shock gives way to anger. Perhaps it is an attempt to reclaim the enslaved or to mete out revenge on the people of the God who has decimated his nation. So his warriors gear up in pursuit of revenge.

Yet as they reach the sea, the waves will part and the pursuing Egyptians will be engulfed by the returning floodwaters. God delivers, and the first exodus is complete.

God, drown the desires of those who would lead us astray
and deliver us from evil. Amen.

GORDON GILES

Unleavened leaving

The Israelites journeyed from Rameses to Succoth, about six hundred thousand men on foot, besides little ones. A mixed crowd also went up with them and livestock in great numbers, both flocks and herds. They baked unleavened cakes of the dough that they had brought out of Egypt; it was not leavened, because they were driven out of Egypt and could not wait, nor had they prepared any provisions for themselves.

The festivals of Passover and of Unleavened Bread both date from the exodus and to some extent have merged, such that the Passover is the first day of a period of seven days during which leaven must not be consumed nor found anywhere in the house (Exodus 12:19; 13:7).

Leaven is yeast, and it makes bread rise. Still today, Passover bread must be unleavened, like this bread the Israelites ate in Egypt before fleeing across the sea to safety. Subsequently, in order to ensure there is no leaven in a house at Passover time, the wife of the home hides some breadcrumbs and the husband, taking a child with him and carrying a candle, searches it out, sweeping it up into a cloth with a wooden spoon and a feather (to avoid being made unclean by it). It is carried in a napkin to the synagogue, where everything is ceremoniously burned.

Leaven represents sin, and thus the home is purged of sin before the commemorative meal can begin. This pre-Passover ritual is known as *Bedikat Chametz*, and there are similarities to be noticed with Shrove Tuesday traditions, whereby unwanted foods, such as eggs, are consumed. Thus sin, or the temptation to sin, is symbolically removed.

The command to eat unleavened bread was fundamentally practical. There will not be time to leaven the bread: just knead it and bake it and eat it. It is the first fast food, a time-saving takeaway. As Christians, we recall a different bread of sustenance, which is also spiritual and physical: the living bread of heaven that is the risen Christ. For in the second exodus, he is the new Moses leading his people through the waters of sin, sustaining them with a bread that is his own body.

God, feed us with the living bread of sincerity and truth,
that is the one and only Jesus Christ our Lord. Amen.

GORDON GILES

Double crossing

Pharaoh king of Egypt... pursued the Israelites... The Lord drove the sea back by a strong east wind all night and turned the sea into dry land, and the waters were divided. The Israelites went into the sea on dry ground, the waters forming a wall for them on their right and on their left. The Egyptians pursued and went into the sea after them... The waters returned and covered... the entire army of Pharaoh that had followed them into the sea; not one of them remained.

The story of Moses crossing the sea lies at the core of preparations for Easter. It is a story of deliverance, escape, rescue and redemption. Jewish tradition commemorates this defining event annually. For Christians there is a deeper meaning relating to the redemption brought by God in Jesus Christ. We only have to think of deliverance from slavery, escape, rescue and redemption to make connections with the fundamental message of the New Testament.

The Old Testament, or covenant, is founded on that relationship created by God with Abraham and Moses, making the Jewish people a chosen people, who were instructed to live by God's commandments ministered to them by Moses. The New Testament, or covenant, is about what is ministered by and through Jesus Christ, who is characterised as a second Adam (1 Corinthians 15:21–22), who cancels out the sin of the fall. He is also a second Moses, who leads his people to freedom by a metaphorical, second exodus. Moses saved the people by leading them across the tempestuous sea by a miracle that is barely believable. In Christ, the seawaters of death become the flowing waters of baptism into new life. The bondage left behind in the second exodus is slavery to sin.

Jesus saves the world by leading us through the darkness of death to resurrection light. He parts the waters of death, by dying and rising again. It is a second exodus – a second and greater deliverance and rescue. It is a wider and deeper sea that Jesus leads us all across: and he does it *on* the cross.

Lead us, heavenly Father, over the world's tempestuous sea. Guard and guide us, keep us, feed us, for we have no help but you, and we possess every blessing, under the wings of your unfailing love. Amen (adapted from 'Lead us, heavenly Father, lead us' by James Edmeston, 1791–1867).

GORDON GILES

Holy Week and Easter

If there is anything that we can learn from reflecting upon the events of Holy Week and Easter, it is that being faithful, prayerful and caring does not protect you from bad things happening. Jesus lived his whole life in the service of God and others, yet he was turned upon by those in positions of power and abandoned by his friends before being executed in a cruel and demeaning way. At the beginning of the week he is treated as a conquering hero, riding into Jerusalem and acclaimed as the Messiah foretold by the prophets. By the end of the week, some of the women who had been most faithful to him are weeping outside his tomb. It is a very short step from being a hero to being – as some thought – yesterday's man.

We live today in a world where technology makes it possible for us to know almost instantly what is happening around the world. Yet at the same time, the nature of digital communication keeps us detached from reality. Instead of speaking to those who have witnessed events, engaging with them in a direct and personal way, we view news on a screen, making it easy to become a passive spectator. It is harder to be compassionate or understanding; it is tempting to join in with the majority view or the loudest voices. Holy Week acts as a warning to us all: beware the power of the mob. Ask, what is really going on when scapegoats are publicly shamed? What are the real issues at play here? Who benefits?

Engaging with Holy Week can be exhausting. If we are truly to travel with Jesus, we need to put ourselves prayerfully and emotionally in his place, viewing through his eyes the adoring crowds who turn against him and cry out, 'Crucify!', the trusted friends who fade away at signs of danger, the cowardice of those in power, and the detachment of those who inflict physical pain and punishment.

We hold on, as he does, to God's eternal presence, even in the midst of such suffering and bewilderment. And we know, of course, that Easter will come. There will be renewal and joy. There is always hope.

AMANDA BLOOR

Who do we see?

Jesus sent two disciples, saying to them, 'Go into the village ahead of you, and immediately you will find a donkey tied and a colt with her; untie them and bring them to me. If anyone says anything to you, just say this, "The Lord needs them." And he will send them immediately.' This took place to fulfil what had been spoken through the prophet: 'Tell the daughter of Zion, Look, your king is coming to you, humble and mounted on a donkey, and on a colt, the foal of a donkey.'

As Jesus travels with his followers, he is often identified in terms of his actions: as teacher, healer, scholar, prophet. This is the moment at which he takes on the identity of Messiah, the king who has been foretold. Jesus was well aware of what he was doing and what the consequences could be; he lived in a country where those with religious influence and military power had formed an uneasy alliance and both factions were likely to see his actions as a threat.

To the crowds, this was a moment of decision too. Were they to support Jesus or to dismiss him as a pretender? As the Bible tells us, they reacted enthusiastically to his entry to Jerusalem on the back of a donkey, calling him 'Son of David' and the one who 'comes in the name of the Lord' (v. 9).

The difficulty with excitement, of course, is that it can quickly die away. Jesus refuses to water down his teaching, continuing to make enemies among the Pharisees. The crowds view him as a freedom fighter; the authorities, as a dangerous revolutionary. There will be trouble ahead.

When we view Jesus, we see him partly through the lens of history, partly through the teaching we have absorbed and partly through our own experience. How we identify him matters – because we know there will always be challenges to our faith. Who do we see when we look at Jesus? Will it help us to remain faithful?

Jesus, you always resisted being labelled by others. Help me to see the fullness of your identity and recognise God at work in and through you. Work in and through me too, I pray. Amen.

AMANDA BLOOR

A last supper

Jesus sent Peter and John… So they went and found everything as he had told them; and they prepared the Passover meal. When the hour came, he took his place at the table, and the apostles with him. He said to them, 'I have eagerly desired to eat this Passover with you before I suffer, for I tell you, I will not eat it until it is fulfilled in the kingdom of God.'

I sometimes wonder what I would do if I knew that the end of my life was near. I think that I would want to spend time with the people I love, perhaps sharing a meal and talking about the things that we had experienced and valued together.

In this passage, we see Jesus doing just that. He knows that death is approaching, so he uses the festival of Passover to gather his friends around a communal table. They slip into the familiar routines – the meal is prepared, bread broken and a cup of wine passed around. They tell their faith history and remember the covenant that God made with their ancestors. Then Jesus adds in a new element. He equates the bread they eat with his body and the wine with his blood. 'Do this to remember me,' he says.

Many of us will have traditions passed down within our families: things that we always do to celebrate Christmas or birthdays, little rituals that ground us, remind us of our past and bind us closer. As time moves on, we might do these things to remind us of those we have lost and to hand on memories to future generations. But what Jesus does at that last Passover supper has an extra depth and significance. He makes a new covenant and opens the way for us all, when we share that bread and wine, to be uniquely close to him. The end becomes a new beginning.

Loving Jesus, thank you for inviting me to share in your last supper, to eat the bread, to drink the wine and to remember you. May I always know that I am welcome at your table, so that I may in turn welcome others into your presence. Amen.

AMANDA BLOOR

Scattered sheep

Jesus said to them, 'You will all fall away, for it is written, "I will strike the shepherd, and the sheep will be scattered." But after I am raised up, I will go before you to Galilee.' Peter said to him, 'Even though all fall away, I will not.' Jesus said to him, 'Truly I tell you, this day, this very night, before the cock crows twice, you will deny me three times.'

Poor Peter. He is confident that he will do better than his fellow disciples, and yet he is so frail under pressure. Jesus' warning is that they will *all* desert him and be scattered like frightened sheep; Peter's recurring failing is that his desire to be Jesus' best friend leads him into making a rash promise that he will be unable to keep. 'They might let you down, but I won't,' he boasts. But all are human and frail, all will fall away – Peter in a way that is particularly public and painful, denying Jesus not once, but three times on the very day he hears that warning.

Jesus knows his disciples well, and he understands their weaknesses. We see throughout the Easter story that they let him down when he needs them most, yet he cares for them still. That is important for each of us to remember too. We do not have to be superhuman or saintly; only God is perfect, and Jesus has already won the battle for us. We need simply to trust and to follow. Unless we believe that we are allowed to fail, we will be paralysed by fear and unable to respond to Christ's calling into his service. Remember this: Jesus knew that his friends would desert him, but he promised nevertheless to go before them when he was 'raised up' and meet them in Galilee. He didn't turn away from them, because he loved them and needed them still. He does not give up and neither should we.

Jesus, you loved your friends regardless of their failings. You kept faith with them. Help us to trust in your love and to live for you, unafraid of our weaknesses. Go before us and greet us as we continue to journey on. Amen.

AMANDA BLOOR

Betrayed with a kiss

While [Jesus] was still speaking, Judas, one of the twelve, arrived; with him was a large crowd with swords and clubs, from the chief priests and the elders of the people. Now the betrayer had given them a sign, saying, 'The one I will kiss is the man; arrest him.' At once he came up to Jesus and said, 'Greetings, Rabbi!' and kissed him. Jesus said to him, 'Friend, do what you are here to do.'

I am sure that each one of us has, at some time, been betrayed by someone we trusted. A friend, a lover, a family member – someone we thought we knew, someone of whom we expected better has badly let us down, and the hurt runs very deep. No matter what the motivation behind the act, no matter how hard we try to understand it, we can be so shaken that our whole sense of self is damaged. Our Christian faith as expressed in the Lord's Prayer encourages us to ask for God's forgiveness 'as we forgive those who sin against us', but forgiveness can, in some situations, be very hard to grant.

I do not know if Jesus was, at that precise moment of betrayal, able to forgive Judas for what he had done, knowing what would follow from it. But I am struck that even as he was surrounded by armed men intent on doing him harm, Jesus was still able to call Judas 'friend'. It was not the actions of the moment, devastating as they were, that identified Judas; he was not called 'traitor' or 'turncoat'. He was 'friend' even though he was not behaving as such.

I imagine that when Judas saw Jesus condemned to death, that word 'friend' must have stung. We know that he bitterly repented of what he had done and tried to give back the 30 pieces of silver he had been paid to betray Jesus. But Jesus had called him friend, and the implication is that despite his actions, whatever his motives, Judas was still loved.

Merciful Lord, I know that there are times when I find it difficult to forgive those who hurt me. Sometimes I find it difficult to forgive myself. Love me still. Amen.

AMANDA BLOOR

Fear and self-loathing

A female servant came to [Peter] and said, 'You also were with Jesus the Galilean.' But he denied it before all of them, saying, 'I do not know what you are talking about.' When he went out to the porch, another female servant saw him, and she said to the bystanders, 'This man was with Jesus the Nazarene.' Again he denied it with an oath, 'I do not know the man.' After a little while the bystanders came up and said to Peter, 'Certainly you are also one of them, for your accent betrays you.' Then he began to curse, and he swore an oath, 'I do not know the man!'

My heart sinks when I read this passage, because I can imagine so clearly how Peter must have felt. Having been warned by Jesus that he would deny him three times before the cock crowed and having been so sure that he would never let down his friend and his teacher, Peter is suddenly overcome with fear. He followed the mob that arrested Jesus all the way to Caiaphas' house, albeit at a distance, and while that was brave, when questioned about his allegiances, Peter's courage drains away. He saves himself from possible arrest as a conspirator, but in doing so, he denies knowing his friend.

There is a warning for all of us in this story not to promise more than we are able to deliver. Peter's earlier bluster – 'They might let you down, but I never will' – is shown to be an empty boast, and Peter is hideously shamed by it. He weeps bitterly. We might say, 'Pride comes before a fall.'

But there is hope for us too. Later in the story, the risen Jesus allows Peter to regain his self-respect and in a more measured way, to express his love for Christ. As a result, he is able to continue to follow his Lord and fulfil his calling. Peter is shown kindness and mercy. God always offers us the same.

Gentle, generous God, help me to know my limitations and to rely upon your strength rather than my own. When I fall, as you know I will, forgive me and lift me up that I may begin again. Amen.

AMANDA BLOOR

Alone and bereft

When it was noon, darkness came over the whole land until three in the afternoon. At three o'clock Jesus cried out with a loud voice, 'Eloi, Eloi, lema sabachthani?' which means, 'My God, my God, why have you forsaken me?' When some of the bystanders heard it, they said, 'Listen, he is calling for Elijah.' And someone ran, filled a sponge with sour wine, put it on a stick, and gave it to him to drink.

Bringing up children isn't easy. Many of us will know how difficult it is to maintain a balance between protecting children from harm and enabling them to grow to be independent. At times, the children we love will say things that feel hurtful, because they are testing boundaries, they are angry or they feel let down. I was told once that such behaviour is a sign that they feel secure enough to express their negative feelings because they know that they are loved.

I find it fascinating that after all the times Jesus described his ministry of God as his Father in heaven, when onlookers heard his anguished outburst from the cross, they couldn't believe that he was referring to God. He had taught, in the Lord's Prayer, that God is *our* Father too, and he had maintained a prayerful intimacy with God. Despite this, hearing the words from the cross, the bystanders assumed that he was calling upon Elijah, hoping that the prophet would come and help. Yet here we have an example of the unguarded relationship between Christ and God. He cries out in pain and distress: 'Why have you left me?'

We can only imagine the depths of Jesus' sense of abandonment at this point. Death is near and he feels very alone. Is he able to trust in God's love at this moment, I wonder? I hope so, even if that belief is expressed in a cry of anger and loss.

God, our heavenly parent, sometimes things happen that make us question your love. It is hard when we suffer or when we see the suffering of others. We may never understand in this life, but help us to hold on to the trust that you love us and will never abandon us. Amen.

AMANDA BLOOR

Creation is outraged

It was now about noon, and darkness came over the whole land until three in the afternoon, while the sun's light failed, and the curtain of the temple was torn in two. Then Jesus, crying out with a loud voice, said, 'Father, into your hands I commend my spirit.' Having said this, he breathed his last. When the centurion saw what had taken place, he praised God and said, 'Certainly this man was innocent.'

In the beginning, as the book of Genesis reminds us, God began the work of creation by making light. Everything else followed on from that moment, as the darkness was broken into by God's light. Yet the crucifixion is such a shocking event that creation itself is impacted. It is midday, the brightest hour, and as Jesus, the light of the world, suffers on the cross for three hours, the sun is blotted out. It feels as if the world, like the curtain of the temple, is being ripped apart. How is it possible to make sense of such a moment?

Momentous events can change those who experience them. We're not told how Pilate, Herod or the chief priests reacted as the land was plunged into darkness. I hope it gave them pause for thought. But for one onlooker, a centurion tasked with overseeing the crucifixion, it is proof that Jesus is innocent of the charges made against him. And more than that, he *praises* God for the insight that he has gained.

I wonder if there have been occasions in our own lives when we have been made to re-evaluate our beliefs and understandings? Perhaps something has happened to us or we have witnessed something happening to others, and we have only been able to begin to understand it, as the centurion did, by turning towards God.

The darkness, of course, did not have the last word. But that comes later in the story. For now, in the space of Easter Eve, we must acknowledge the reality of darkness and our constant need for God's presence.

Almighty God, who began creation with light, remind us that your light has never been overcome by darkness. Illuminate our lives, especially when we cannot clearly see the light. Amen.

AMANDA BLOOR

'Who is it you are looking for?'

[Mary] saw two angels in white, seated where Jesus' body had been... They asked her, 'Woman, why are you crying?' 'They have taken my Lord away,' she said, 'and I don't know where they have put him.' At this, she turned round and saw Jesus standing there, but she did not realise that it was Jesus. He asked her, 'Woman, why are you crying? Who is it you are looking for?' Thinking he was the gardener, she said, 'Sir, if you have carried him away, tell me where you have put him, and I will get him.'

Mary Magdalene has always been faithful to Jesus, the person who showed her love and gave her back her self-respect. She is named as one of the women standing by the cross as he suffers and dies, and as soon as the sabbath is over, she goes to pay her respects at his tomb. But his resting place appears to have been desecrated and, finally broken by this last indignity, she weeps.

We know, as she does not yet know, that there is good news: Jesus is risen from the dead. The angels guarding the tomb ask her, as Jesus also does, 'Why are you crying?' But Jesus then asks a question that strikes at the very heart of our faith: 'Who is it you are looking for?'

I wonder who it is that we look for when we turn towards Christ. A holy man? A wise teacher? A healer? A miracle worker? A faithful friend? The Son of God? Or God's own self? We find Jesus described in all these ways and more throughout the Bible. We are encouraged, as we read the Easter story, to remember that Christ was fully human – he suffered, he loved, he laughed, he wept and he died – but is also revealed to us as divine. He has overcome death and pointed us towards heaven. When we search for him in our daily lives, as I hope we do, who is it that we look for?

Jesus, Saviour, Messiah, Word of God, light in our darkness, our constant hope, be with us today and each day as we negotiate our way in this troubled and beautiful world. Help us to see you as you are and to trust you always. Amen.

AMANDA BLOOR

Building a future

Mary Magdalene went and announced to the disciples, 'I have seen the Lord,' and she told them that he had said these things to her. When it was evening on that day, the first day of the week, and the doors were locked where the disciples were, for fear of the Jews, Jesus came and stood among them and said, 'Peace be with you.' After he had said this, he showed them his hands and his side.

It is not surprising that the disciples still locked themselves away out of fear, even after Mary has told them about her encounter with the risen Christ. They saw Pilate offering to set Jesus free, sensing that the chief priests were acting in their own interests, and the reaction of the crowd who demanded the release of the convicted criminal, Barabbas. Then, when Pilate offered again to release Jesus, the cry went up, 'Crucify him!'

What is going on here, I wonder, that made people react with such violence? It is partly political, with powerful people abusing their influence to sway the opinions of others to serve their own ends. If Jesus continued to gather disciples, his followers could have jeopardised the comfortable lifestyle of the religious elite. Some of it was caused by the tendency to join in with the majority – if people shout loudly enough, there will be those who give credence to their opinions. We see that today in social media 'influencers' who feed their own egos (and bank accounts) by targeting and manipulating those who feel disenfranchised. And some people were excited by the thought of violence and punishment being meted out at their instigation.

So how do we resist this sort of 'groupthink'? Perhaps we need to work to shape a culture where all people feel that they are valued and where good actions, rather than evil behaviours, are commended. In short, we need to grow goodness.

Come, Holy Spirit, and fill our hearts with your wisdom and strength.
Help us to build a world where goodness flourishes
and evil behaviours are resisted. Amen.

AMANDA BLOOR

He goes ahead

'Go quickly and tell his disciples, "He has been raised from the dead, and indeed he is going ahead of you to Galilee; there you will see him." This is my message for you.' So they left the tomb quickly with fear and great joy and ran to tell his disciples. Suddenly Jesus met them and said, 'Greetings!' And they came to him, took hold of his feet, and worshipped him. Then Jesus said to them, 'Do not be afraid; go and tell my brothers and sisters to go to Galilee; there they will see me.'

What is apparent in this story is that there is no standing still in discipleship. The day that we now know as Easter Eve gives a pause point between the death and resurrection of Jesus, but as soon as he is risen from the dead, Jesus is on the move. And he expects the same of his followers.

Jesus does not wait around outside the empty tomb or return to the upper room where he last met with his closest friends. He sends a message via the women who have gone to mourn him that he will be found in Galilee, the place where his ministry first began, a reminder perhaps that those who were called there to follow him have not been released from that obligation. Although some of his disciples do not recognise him immediately and some are doubtful, they all still have tasks to fulfil.

Easter poses that same challenge to each of us too. With Jesus' reassurance ringing in our ears, we are called to not be afraid, but to head off, knowing that Christ goes ahead of us. When we draw near to him, the great commission he gives to the eleven disciples is a message for us too: 'Go and make disciples of all nations' (Matthew 28:19). We are an Easter people; we believe in new beginnings and boundless possibilities. We have good news to share.

Risen Lord Jesus, I believe and trust in you. Go ahead of me, help me to not be afraid, let me share the good news with those who do not yet know your love. I would be your disciple. Fill me with your strength. Amen.

AMANDA BLOOR

Stay with us

As they came near the village to which they were going, he walked ahead as if he were going on. But they urged him strongly, saying, 'Stay with us, because it is almost evening and the day is now nearly over.' So he went in to stay with them. When he was at the table with them, he took bread, blessed and broke it, and gave it to them. Then their eyes were opened.

The two disciples who walk towards the village of Emmaus are not expecting to meet Jesus. Indeed, they spend time explaining to him why they look downcast, how their friend the 'mighty prophet' has been crucified, and how a tale of an empty tomb has been told to them by the women of their group. So when they urge their fellow traveller to stay with them for the night, it is out of concern for his safety – travelling in the dark is dangerous – rather than because they recognise him. But their actions echo those of Mary when she recognised the risen Christ in the garden and was told, 'Don't try to hold on to me.'

The days after Easter are a curious mix of joyful revelation and anxious uncertainty. It will not be until the Day of Pentecost that the disciples will feel fully prepared to continue their mission; they have been used to having Jesus with them, a constant, reassuring presence. It is only natural that they want him to stay.

I am reminded when I read the Easter story that discipleship has always involved the whole faith community. Jesus gathered a group around him who each had a part to play and who supported each other. The disciples in this story travel together, not apart. There will be times when each of us feels uncertain and insufficient for the task ahead, even if we hope that God will be in it. That is when we need others most.

Christ my redeemer and enabler, help me not to hold onto you solely out of fear. Send me the encouragers I need and help me in turn to support my brothers and sisters in faith. Build us up that we may be strong in service and in love. Amen.

AMANDA BLOOR

Integrity and injustice

After the priests had assembled with the elders, they devised a plan to give a large sum of money to the soldiers, telling them, 'You must say, "His disciples came by night and stole him away while we were asleep." If this comes to the governor's ears, we will satisfy him and keep you out of trouble.' So they took the money and did as they were directed. And this story is still told.

What would you do if you were encouraged to take part in a cover-up? Your conscience might tell you to do the right thing, but what if you were approached by people who held immense power, had influential friends and used violence? Or if you knew that any attempt to change the narrative would be used against you, either in a domestic setting or in a fraudulent judicial system? In such a situation, you might take the easier option.

At Jesus' trial, he knew that the charges against him were false and that the witnesses against him were giving contradictory accounts. Even Pilate recognised that the chief priests were motivated by jealousy and that their charges of blasphemy were tenuous. Yet Jesus stood firm, refusing to engage with injustice. The soldiers who had guarded his tomb were pragmatic. When told what to say to protect those who had put Christ to death, they took the money and did as they were ordered.

We might wish that corruption like this could not happen today, but human rights organisations suggest that there are many people around the world who are wrongly imprisoned, suffer abuse, are silenced, become victims of summary punishment or simply disappear. Some are known as 'prisoners of conscience' who have criticised corrupt regimes but have never advocated violence or hatred as a response. Jesus' steadfastness in the face of extreme threat should inspire us to advocate on behalf of the voiceless and powerless. They are loved by God.

Jesus, you stood with dignity and courage in front of those who wished you harm. Help me to stand up for those who suffer today, in the faith that God's kingdom of justice and righteousness is drawing near. Amen.

AMANDA BLOOR

Remaining steadfast

They crucified him there, along with the criminals – one on his right, the other on his left. Jesus said, 'Father, forgive them, for they do not know what they are doing.' And they divided up his clothes by casting lots. The people stood watching, and the rulers even sneered at him. They said, 'He saved others; let him save himself if he is God's Messiah, the Chosen One.' The soldiers also came up and mocked him. They offered him wine vinegar and said, 'If you are the king of the Jews, save yourself.'

A week on from the crucifixion we look back and consider its impact on our own lives. It was bad enough for Jesus to be falsely accused and arrested by corrupt officials. It was unjust to be condemned without a fair trial and without anyone to defend him. It was inhumane to be tortured and then made to carry the instrument of his execution through the streets. It was outrageous that his sentence was carried out in public. How did he, I wonder, maintain his dignity and strength?

By the time that Jesus was crucified, he must have been exhausted. He had been at the Passover meal with his friends, he had stayed awake in the garden to pray, he had been interrogated all night by Caiaphas the high priest and then, in the morning, taken to Pilate. And before his crucifixion, he had been flogged. Most people would have no reserves left.

All this was followed by more indignity and a final temptation. Jesus, in prayer in the garden at Gethsemane, admitted to God that he was afraid. So when he was mocked by those who had brought him to Golgotha, it was both insult and test. 'Prove yourself by saving yourself,' the leaders and soldiers taunted. It was a calculatedly shocking moment.

I am sure that I would not have had the strength of character and courage shown by Jesus. But I can follow his example when I face times of trial by throwing myself completely upon God's mercy, praying for the strength I know that I lack.

God, ground of my being, be with me when I call upon you in prayer.
Never forsake me. Be my hope in times of trouble
and my comfort when I am in need. Amen.

AMANDA BLOOR

The Word made flesh

He was in the world, and the world came into being through him, yet the world did not know him. He came to what was his own, and his own people did not accept him. But to all who received him, who believed in his name, he gave power to become children of God, who were born, not of blood or of the will of the flesh or of the will of man, but of God. And the Word became flesh and lived among us.

We usually hear this passage at Christmas rather than Easter, but for me it is one of the most poetic and powerful statements of faith in the gospels, summing up all that Holy Week and Easter teach us about Jesus' life, death and resurrection. As we considered on Easter Eve, when we thought about the dimming of the sun as Jesus hung on the cross, Christ was present as the creative Word of God from the very beginning of existence and is intimately entwined with the world. When he 'became flesh' at the incarnation and grew to manhood and ministry, it became abundantly clear that he was not accepted by members of his own community and was rejected by those he longed to save. Yet he was not deterred. His entry into Jerusalem to shouts of 'Hosanna' fulfilled earlier prophecies and began the chain of events that led to the cross, and that brief dimming of the light that came to save us from darkness.

As children of God, those of us who receive Christ into our lives know that there will be many occasions where we are faced with death, whether that is literal or metaphorical. We may have to set aside long-held desires, deal with the loss of loved ones, see institutions and relationships swept away. It is always painful. But Easter shows us resurrection: God brings new life to birth; we are loved; there is hope.

Fill us, Holy Spirit, with the strength to carry on in times of darkness and the wisdom to rest in God's loving presence when we feel overwhelmed or anxious. Help us to proclaim Christ's resurrection and to carry his light into this damaged world. Make us resurrection people and bearers of hope. Amen.

AMANDA BLOOR

Resurrection hope: John 11—12

John 11—12 capture the heart of Jesus' mission and show us some of his most dramatic moments. They are full of emotion: grief, love, anger, hope, envy and sacrifice. Through them we see that Jesus has power over life and death, but also is willing to give up his own life for us. You may find it helpful to read through both chapters in full before we begin.

In John 11 we engage with the story of the raising of Lazarus from the dead. In the exchanges that Jesus has with the sisters of Lazarus, we catch a glimpse both of his humanity and his divinity. Jesus weeps with Mary for his friend and tells Martha: 'I am the resurrection and the life.' In heart-breaking situations, Jesus weeps with us and promises to bring new life from the most wretched of places. We can trust Jesus to have both human compassion and divine authority. We see the power of God at work bringing new life from death.

The story is a trailer for the events of Good Friday and Easter Day. God's power extends over all things, even death itself. We are invited to trust that with God no situation is hopeless, and there is nothing that cannot be redeemed.

In John 12 we move from the miracle of new life to the mystery of sacrifice. Mary anoints Jesus with expensive perfume – another precursor for the moment when the body of Jesus will lie in the tomb. Such extravagant love points to the sacrifice that Jesus will make when he lays down his life for us.

Next, we follow Jesus on his journey into Jerusalem as he walks the way of the Messiah. Those who are longing to meet him come close and find that the truest way to see Jesus is to look to the cross, finding beyond its horrors love and life transformed.

Exploring these chapters takes on a deeper significance as we engage with them during this Easter season. Viewed through the lens of Jesus' death and resurrection we see afresh Jesus' power over life and death and the significance of his sacrifice. As we walk this week with Jesus, we are invited to consider our faith in the light of his loving words and actions.

CATHERINE WILLIAMS

Disrupted plans

Now a certain man was ill, Lazarus of Bethany, the village of Mary and her sister Martha… So the sisters sent a message to Jesus, 'Lord, he whom you love is ill.' But when Jesus heard it, he said, 'This illness does not lead to death; rather, it is for God's glory, so that the Son of God may be glorified through it.' Accordingly, though Jesus loved Martha and her sister and Lazarus, after having heard that Lazarus was ill, he stayed two days longer in the place where he was.

How do you react when plans are changed or disrupted? Changing tack requires much effort and some people find this very difficult. Others sit light to events, going with the flow, embracing sudden surprising upheavals with curiosity and a sense of adventure. I have been in the first camp for much of my life, needing to plan thoroughly and getting stressed when plans are derailed. More recently I have been working at letting go of control and being open to what emerges. God can work in amazing and brilliant ways when we leave outcomes open, trusting God to act for good.

Despite hearing the message from the sisters that the friend he loves is ill, Jesus does not rush to Bethany to be with Lazarus, Mary and Martha. He seems certain that Lazarus' illness will not lead to death; he says as much to the disciples. But he also seems to know that somehow God will be revealed through this event. Later in this chapter, when Jesus hears that Lazarus has died, he says he is glad that he did not rush to see him because an occasion for deeper belief has opened up. Jesus recognises the disaster of his friend's death as an opportunity for the glory of God to be revealed. As we will see later this week, Jesus is deeply moved by the death of Lazarus. At the same time, he holds on to hope that something good will emerge. The story of Lazarus, with its echoes of Easter, encourages us to keep trusting in God. Amid the harsh realities of disrupted plans, grief and disaster awaits new life. Death does not have the last word for the Lord of Life.

Lord, help me to trust in your promise of new life. Amen.

CATHERINE WILLIAMS

I Am

Now Bethany was near Jerusalem, some two miles away... When Martha heard that Jesus was coming, she went and met him, while Mary stayed at home. Martha said to Jesus, 'Lord, if you had been here, my brother would not have died. But even now I know that God will give you whatever you ask of him.' Jesus said to her, 'Your brother will rise again.' Martha said to him, 'I know that he will rise again in the resurrection on the last day.' Jesus said to her, 'I am the resurrection and the life.'

Jesus suggests that the death of Lazarus opens the way for deeper belief in God. Martha's response to Jesus confirms this. Though heartbroken at her brother's death, Martha has faith that Lazarus will rise at the resurrection of the dead at the end of earthly time and that God will respond positively to Jesus' requests now. She has hope for the future and a deep longing for God to act in the present.

Responding to Martha, Jesus makes an astonishing declaration: 'I am the resurrection and the life.' Jesus has spoken several 'I am' statements already: 'I am the light of the world' (John 8:12); 'I am the bread of life' (John 6:35); and (the one that got everyone really riled) 'Before Abraham was, I am' (John 8:58), suggesting that he is the God of Israel, the great I AM.

Announcing himself as the resurrection and the life encourages even greater faith from Martha. She boldly declares Jesus to be the Messiah. Soon we will see Jesus demonstrate life-giving power in his interaction with Lazarus. It will be a spoiler alert for what is to come fully in Jesus' death and resurrection. Martha's deep relationship with Jesus means that even amid her grief and disappointment she is filled with hope and belief in God's power to act.

When our lives are rocked by loss, it can be helpful to ponder how we are experiencing God amid the challenges we are facing. Can we hold on to the hope that the future is God-shaped? Jesus walks with us, declaring himself to be the one who brings new life, encouraging us to embrace deeper faith and trust.

'Thine be the glory, risen, conqu'ring Son; endless is the vict'ry thou o'er death hast won' (Edmond Budry, 1854–1932). Amen.

CATHERINE WILLIAMS

Where were you?

When Mary came where Jesus was and saw him, she knelt at his feet and said to him, 'Lord, if you had been here, my brother would not have died.' When Jesus saw her weeping… he was greatly disturbed in spirit and deeply moved. He said, 'Where have you laid him?' They said to him, 'Lord, come and see.' Jesus began to weep. So the Jews said, 'See how he loved him!' But some of them said, 'Could not he who opened the eyes of the blind man have kept this man from dying?'

When challenging things happen to us – accidents, illness, the death of loved ones, losses or catastrophes – it is not unusual to question God: 'Where were you? Why didn't you look out for me? Why did you allow this to happen? We thought you loved us!' People have been questioning God since time began, accusing God of failure, betrayal and hard-heartedness: holding God to account.

Martha did it in the passage yesterday. Mary does it again today. If only Jesus had been there, Lazarus would not have died. There are no easy answers, but expressions of anger and disappointment are healthy. God knows what we think and feel and the heartfelt words we express keep our relationship with God lively and honest.

Jesus gives Mary no answer. There is no apology for not coming sooner. Instead, he turns his attention to Lazarus, asking to see his grave. There, in solidarity with the sisters and those gathered to mourn, Jesus weeps. There is much that we do not know about death, but we do know that in Jesus, God weeps with us, feeling the pain of loss. The Lord who cries is the same Lord who resurrects. The Lord who feels our pain is the same Lord who brings new life out of deadly situations. Death and loss are not the end of our story, they are a place through which we are all called to journey on the way to eternity. As we experience death and loss Jesus is alongside weeping with us, waiting to call us into a new future with him.

'Even though I walk through the valley of the shadow of death, I will fear no evil, for you are with me' (Psalm 23:4a, ESV).

CATHERINE WILLIAMS

Release

Jesus said, 'Take away the stone.' Martha, the sister of the dead man, said to him, 'Lord, already there is a stench because he has been dead for four days.' Jesus said to her, 'Did I not tell you that if you believed you would see the glory of God?' So they took away the stone. And Jesus looked upward and said, 'Father, I thank you for having heard me...' When he had said this, he cried with a loud voice, 'Lazarus, come out!' The dead man came out, his hands and feet bound with strips of cloth and his face wrapped in a cloth. Jesus said to them, 'Unbind him, and let him go.'

The trappings of death bind us tightly. Loss and grief take us into airless places where we struggle to breathe and where we are not sure which way to turn. The world we know shrinks and turns in on itself like a tomb. The death of someone we love can do this to us. But other losses, too, tie our hands and hearts, forcing us into a shape and space from which it seems hard to escape.

Jesus asks for the tomb of Lazarus to be opened. Martha expects the stench of decay to come flooding out but the essential 'aliveness' of Jesus – the Lord of life – calls Lazarus back from the grave and out into the fresh air of new life. Lazarus is still wearing the winding cloths which bind him tightly. Jesus asks his family and friends to take these grave clothes from him, releasing him to live again.

As Christians, we are called to witness to new life in Jesus. The grave is not the end but the gateway to a spacious new way of living beyond anything we can imagine. During our time on earth, Jesus is always calling us into new life, new ways of seeing and being that bring life and joy to ourselves and others. Jesus calls us out of a constricted existence into expansive life in all its fullness. Let us resolve to unbind each other from the deadly things that trap us and encourage God's new life to flow through us.

Lord, roll away the stone and release me into new life. Amen.

CATHERINE WILLIAMS

Fragrant devotion

Six days before the Passover Jesus came to Bethany, the home of Lazarus, whom he had raised from the dead. There they gave a dinner for him. Martha served, and Lazarus was one of those reclining with him. Mary took a pound of costly perfume made of pure nard, anointed Jesus' feet, and wiped them with her hair. The house was filled with the fragrance of the perfume. But Judas Iscariot, one of his disciples (the one who was about to betray him), said, 'Why was this perfume not sold for three hundred denarii and the money given to the poor?'

Bethany is Jesus' happy place. This family home, just outside Jerusalem, is a haven where he can rest and renew his energy and resolve. For Mary, Martha and Lazarus, Jesus has become incredibly special. He has restored Lazarus to life. The siblings throw a celebratory party for Jesus. Imagine this home, filled with warmth, laughter and the love of friends, brought together by God who makes the impossible possible, bringing triumph from tragedy.

Martha offers her gift of hospitality, and Mary anoints Jesus' feet with the most expensive, exquisite perfume money can buy. What an act of devotion! Mary is anointing the anointed one – the Christ. Imagine the sweet fragrance filling the house. Breathe in the heady, delicious scent. The moment is intense and intimate. As Mary breaks open the jar and pours out its rich and costly contents, Jesus pours out himself for everyone. The fragrant, loving sacrifice of Christ fills the whole world.

Sadly, there are other odours at Bethany. Just below the surface, in the mounting tension, is the scent of something rotten and deadly. Can you smell it? Judas is trying to grab the moral high ground, asking why the perfume was wasted on Jesus when the money could have been given to the poor. Is he envious? Does he long to anoint the feet of Jesus too but fears the intimacy? The scent of betrayal and untimely death is lingering in the shadows waiting to pounce.

We know how the story plays out and which scent ultimately prevails. As we celebrate the resurrection, on this day in Eastertide, what is the fragrance of your response to Jesus?

May the fragrance of Jesus fill this place. Amen.

CATHERINE WILLIAMS

In hindsight

The next day the great crowd that had come to the festival heard that Jesus was coming to Jerusalem. So they took branches of palm trees and went out to meet him, shouting, 'Hosanna! Blessed is the one who comes in the name of the Lord – the King of Israel!' Jesus found a young donkey and sat on it, as it is written: 'Do not be afraid, daughter of Zion. Look, your king is coming, sitting on a donkey's colt!' His disciples did not understand these things at first, but when Jesus was glorified, then they remembered that these things had been written of him and had been done to him.

Hindsight is a wonderful thing! Confusion, bewilderment and frustration may happen in the present, but looking back we see patterns emerging and make sense of events. 'Life can only be understood backwards, but it must be lived forwards,' wrote the Danish philosopher Søren Kierkegaard (1813–55). The disciples only put the jigsaw together after the death and resurrection of Jesus. At the time they were caught up in living the events.

And such events! Crowds waving palm branches, shouting welcome to the king of Israel, who they hoped would liberate them from the Romans. 'Hosanna!' they cry, 'Save us, Jesus!' A great moment of drama unites the onlookers. Soon they will be united in condemning Jesus and baying for his blood. How quickly a crowd can turn.

Jesus comes into Jerusalem humbly on a young donkey. It is not the regal entry of a king or conqueror. He comes from the Mount of Olives, across the Kidron Valley and through the Golden Gate in the eastern wall. This way into the city is also called the Gate of Mercy. It is the gate through which the Messiah is expected to enter the temple. Jesus is re-enacting the prophecy from Zechariah, but it is only later that people will make the connections.

As you look back over your journey of faith, can you see how God has been preparing you to welcome Jesus? How and where did you first encounter him, and who is he for you now? What is your cry as you welcome the risen Christ today?

'Blessed is he who comes in the name of the Lord' (Psalm 118:26, NIV).

CATHERINE WILLIAMS

Seeing Jesus

Now among those who went up to worship at the festival were some Greeks. They came to Philip, who was from Bethsaida in Galilee, and said to him, 'Sir, we wish to see Jesus'... Andrew and Philip went and told Jesus. Jesus answered them, 'The hour has come for the Son of Man to be glorified. Very truly, I tell you, unless a grain of wheat falls into the earth and dies, it remains just a single grain, but if it dies, it bears much fruit.'

Why do the Greek visitors to Jerusalem wish to see Jesus? With the miracles, healings, confrontations with the religious authorities, and raising of Lazarus, Jesus is becoming a celebrity. No wonder they want to see him. I want to see this Jesus too! Do you?

Jesus responds by announcing his destiny. His hour has come, and he illustrates this with a picture from the natural world. Abundant life from death. This is the principle that God has hard-wired into the universe. When death leads to life, God is revealed.

So, to see Jesus truly and to understand who he is, the visitors to Jerusalem, the disciples and we should look to the cross. Dying for each of us, Jesus draws us to himself and the glory of God is fully revealed. In our celebrity culture, fame, status, honour and wealth matter most. But God's glory is seen in defeat, humiliation, servanthood and self-sacrifice. It is this way of dying and living that bears fruit.

Seeing Jesus, then, is not a spectator sport, like royal watching or celebrity hunting. Seeing Jesus is a way to follow, a truth to embody and a life to live. We see Jesus by letting go, emptying, dying to self and allowing new life to arise.

Our world is full of those who need to see Jesus. Do they see Jesus in us, his followers and friends who journey with him, walk in his footsteps and follow his way? This Eastertide who can you encourage to meet with the risen Lord, who has endured the cross, conquered death and longs to lead all into new life?

'He who on the cross a victim, for the world's salvation bled,
Jesus Christ, the King of glory, now is risen from the dead'
(Christopher Wordsworth, 1807–85).

CATHERINE WILLIAMS

Resurrection

Easter Sunday was two weeks ago, but we are still in the Easter season! Quite naturally, around Easter itself we tend to concentrate mostly on the gospel accounts of the events leading up to the crucifixion, death, burial and resurrection of Jesus. By looking specifically at Jesus' resurrection, we gain a good overview from the gospel accounts. But what did the Jewish people in the Old Testament and at the time of Jesus think about death and resurrection? Was what happened to Jesus what they might have expected, and if not, how was it different? Then, after the resurrection, what did the early church think? Did they have everything worked out or were there still areas of uncertainty?

To investigate these questions, we will first look at the Old Testament, specifically Ezekiel 37 and Daniel 12. Then we will move on to 1 Corinthians 15, one of the most in-depth discussions of the implications of Jesus' resurrection in the New Testament.

This can all sound very theoretical, the realm of theologians, and not at all of interest to most people. However, the Cambridge Dictionary has this good definition of resurrection: 'In the Christian religion, the Resurrection is Jesus Christ's return to life on the third day after his death, or the return of all people to life at the end of the world.' The resurrection does not just involve Jesus, but all of us. The Bible clearly tells us that Jesus was the firstfruits of the resurrection (1 Corinthians 15:20). So in simple terms, what happened to him will also happen to us! If that is the case, then the resurrection surely must be of interest to everyone.

The funeral service says, 'Earth to earth, ashes to ashes, dust to dust; in sure and certain hope of the Resurrection to eternal life, through our Lord Jesus Christ.' That means we should expect to be resurrected. But how will this happen? When might it happen? Where will we end up after we are resurrected? Will we be in heaven or somewhere else? What kind of bodies will we have? Will our sadly degraded environment also be restored? All kinds of questions! This week we will try to unpack some of them for you.

MARTIN AND MARGOT HODSON

The valley of the bones

The hand of the Lord was on me, and he brought me out by the Spirit of the Lord and set me in the middle of a valley; it was full of bones. He led me to and fro among them, and I saw a great many bones on the floor of the valley, bones that were very dry. He asked me, 'Son of man, can these bones live?' I said, 'Sovereign Lord, you alone know.'

I once visited Sudbury in northern Ontario, Canada. It was famous for its nickel and copper mining activity, which had led to whole areas around the city being seriously degraded, particularly in the first half of the last century. We wandered across a previously forested area that had become a blackened rock desert. Just a few tufts of tough grass survived in this inhospitable environment. The whitened, dead stumps of the trees that once grew there were markers of what once was. The valley of the bones reminds me of the Sudbury wastelands, with the dead trees representing the bones.

The book of Ezekiel was written during the exile in Babylon, and today's passage comes towards the end, where the prophet is looking forward to the restoration of Israel. It is uncertain what the Jewish people of the time thought about the afterlife and resurrection. The majority of scholars suggest that the Israelites assumed that after death they would enter Sheol, a kind of underworld where both good and bad people go upon dying. It's not until the period after the exile that we see evidence that any type of resurrection was much in the Jewish mindset. However, some recent writers have suggested that resurrection thinking is implied in some of the Psalms and in Isaiah, even if it is not made explicit.

When we visited Sudbury, our party was also shown areas where revegetation projects had been initiated, led by scientists at Laurentian University. In some places it was impossible to tell how bad things once were. It was a kind of environmental resurrection – the bones could live.

Pray for all those who 'bring bones to life', through restoration projects of places that have been badly damaged.

MARTIN HODSON

'Dem bones'

Then he said to me, 'Prophesy to these bones and say to them, "Dry bones, hear the word of the Lord! This is what the Sovereign Lord says to these bones: I will make breath enter you, and you will come to life. I will attach tendons to you and make flesh come upon you and cover you with skin; I will put breath in you, and you will come to life. Then you will know that I am the Lord."'

I cannot read this passage without thinking back to the song from my childhood 'Dem bones', with its chorus 'Dem bones, dem bones, dem dry bones, Hear the word of the Lord' and verse 'Toe bone connected to the foot bone, foot bone connected to the heel bone, heel bone connected to the ankle bone…' This spiritual song, based on Ezekiel's prophecy, was originally written in the 1920s by the Johnson brothers. James Weldon Johnson was an African American leader of the civil rights movement, and his brother, J. Rosamond Johnson, was a composer and singer.

At first sight, today's passage seems to be talking about the resurrection of people. Indeed, it has sometimes been read at funerals and understood as an assurance of life after death. However, it is clear from Ezekiel 37:11–12 that it mainly concerns the restoration of the Jewish people to Israel after their exile in Babylon: 'These bones are the people of Israel… My people, I am going to open your graves and bring you up from them; I will bring you back to the land of Israel.' Ezekiel's vision was that God's downtrodden people would endure; it was not individual people that were to be resurrected, but Israel itself.

We cannot get inside the heads of the Johnson brothers when they wrote 'Dem bones', but it feels like they were thinking about justice, restoration and, yes, a resurrection for their people. Ezekiel 37 became a popular text for African American preachers in the late 19th century when the Johnsons would have heard it as children. Were the brothers, very subtly, relating the captivity of the Jewish people in Babylon to their own situation in the United States? I think they were.

Pray for all those around the world who are fighting against racial discrimination.

MARTIN HODSON

The archangel Michael

'At that time Michael, the great prince who protects your people, will arise. There will be a time of distress such as has not happened from the beginning of nations until then. But at that time your people – everyone whose name is found written in the book – will be delivered. Multitudes who sleep in the dust of the earth will awake: some to everlasting life, others to shame and everlasting contempt.'

For five years, Margot was chaplain of Jesus College, Oxford. Hanging in the sanctuary of Jesus College Chapel is a large copy of *The Archangel Michael Defeating Satan*, a painting by Guido Reni. The original painting is in Santa Maria della Concezione dei Cappuccini, Rome. Imagine a warlike figure holding a sword and with his left foot on the devil's head and you will have the idea. Michael is the chief of the angels, and was particularly responsible for the protection of Israel. He first appears in the Bible in Daniel 10:13 as 'one of the chief princes', but is also prominent in the non-canonical book of Enoch and reappears in the New Testament in Jude and Revelation.

The book of Daniel begins with familiar narrative material, including the furnace and the lion's den, and ends with complex prophetic writings. The book is set in the sixth century BC, but was probably written in the second century BC during the time of the Maccabees, a group of rebel Jewish warriors who overthrew the Seleucids and captured Jerusalem. It was a turbulent period of history, and apocalyptic writings like Enoch and Daniel captured the imaginations of those living at the time.

It is significant that Michael is there at the beginning of this passage to protect and guide the people at a time of great turmoil. The prophecy predicts that the Jewish people, at least those written about in a book, will be delivered. At that time the dead will awaken, and they will be divided, with some gaining everlasting life and others everlasting contempt. This is the first absolutely clear account of resurrection in the Bible, and moreover it is the first indication of a future judgement. Evidently, thinking about resurrection was changing as we neared the end of the Old Testament.

Give thanks for the resurrection to eternal life.

MARTIN HODSON

The end of the days

'From the time that the daily sacrifice is abolished and the abomination that causes desolation is set up, there will be 1,290 days. Blessed is the one who waits for and reaches the end of the 1,335 days. As for you, go your way till the end. You will rest, and then at the end of the days you will rise to receive your allotted inheritance.'

While we were writing these reflections, we heard the news that Hal Lindsey, the American Christian writer and television host, had died at the age of 95. Lindsey was best known as the author of *The Late Great Planet Earth*, which first appeared in 1970 and sold millions of copies. I went on a hunt through our bookshelves and found a battered copy that had somehow survived various previous book culls, probably because of its historic interest. It is a book of prophecies, where Lindsey uses the Bible to interpret current events and to predict the future, particularly the end of the world. Lindsey made a fortune on book sales, but all his predictions proved to be incorrect.

Not surprisingly, Lindsey made a lot of use of the book of Daniel in his prophetic writings. There is much speculation about the meaning of today's passage, the final verses of the book. Verses 11–12 seem to refer to a time when temple worship is restored and is then abolished again, but the significance of 1,290 days and 1,335 days is obscure.

For us the most important verse is the last (v. 13). It indicates that there will be a time of rest, presumably for those who have died, followed by an 'end of the days', indicating that this world as we know it will end. At that time the dead will rise to receive their 'allotted inheritance'. This suggests that those who have risen will be rewarded in some way.

By the time of Daniel, it is clear that many Jewish people believed in a bodily resurrection at the end of time, and that this would involve judgement. These themes were considerably developed in the New Testament, to which we will turn next.

Pray that we may be given wisdom
in interpreting complex passages like Daniel 12.

MARTIN HODSON

Trustworthy accounts

For what I received I passed on to you as of first importance: that Christ died for our sins according to the Scriptures, that he was buried, that he was raised on the third day according to the Scriptures, and that he appeared to Cephas, and then to the Twelve. After that, he appeared to more than five hundred of the brothers and sisters at the same time.

My parents grew up in Bristol during World War II. When we were children, they would tell us stories of their experiences. One of those was how, on the morning after Bristol was bombed, my dad carried on as normal, walking into the city centre to go to school, which he expected to be open as usual; even though he had to climb over rubble to get to school, he was surprised to find it closed. They were extraordinary times, and my parents never forgot the details of their experiences. Many years later, my dad was in a nursing home and was asked to write his memories of the war. He wrote down that same story.

Our reading today is thought to be the earliest account of the resurrection, written before any of the gospels. It sets out the heart of the Christian faith, that Christ died for our sins, that he was raised from the dead and that there were many witnesses to this. Cephas is Aramaic for Peter and would mostly likely have been the name that Jesus used for him. Paul preserves the name to keep his account exactly as he had heard it.

But he did not just pass on what he had heard. Paul had also reflected on Christ's death and resurrection from his considerable knowledge of the Hebrew scriptures. He had come to the firm conclusion that the eyewitness accounts fitted with the biblical prophecies. He had no doubt that Jesus was the Messiah and had been raised from the dead.

Today, we live in an age where truth has become obscured by multiple layers of technology. It can be hard to know what is real. In the end, the best way is to hear an eyewitness account from someone we trust. Today we can trust in the authenticity of the resurrection accounts from those first disciples and trust that Jesus is indeed the Saviour of the world.

Pray that the Lord will help us to trust and follow him all our days.

MARGOT HODSON

Christ, the firstfruits

If it is preached that Christ has been raised from the dead, how can some of you say that there is no resurrection of the dead?... But Christ has indeed been raised from the dead, the firstfruits of those who have fallen asleep... For as in Adam all die, so in Christ all will be made alive. But each in turn: Christ, the firstfruits; then, when he comes, those who belong to him.

In the first spring that we spent in our last vicarage, we were delighted to see blossom on an old fruit tree that was also providing a home in its trunk to a family of blue tits. A few weeks later and just in time, we discovered its 'unripe' green plums were in fact very ripe greengages – they were delicious!

The firstfruits in this passage are from the barley harvest. Barley was the first to be harvested of seven biblical fruits that were offered in the temple each year. On the second day of Passover, a sheaf was cut and presented as a wave offering. If we follow the timings of John's gospel, this firstfruits offering would have been on the morning of Easter Sunday. Christ had risen indeed!

As Christians we are used to faith connecting with eternal life and it can be a surprise to learn that many in the ancient world, including residents of Corinth, did not believe in an afterlife apart from a very hazy eternal rest in an underworld. Even believing, we can also be hazy about eternal life in a vague upper realm. It can be a surprise to us to discover that the New Testament focus is on actual resurrection. All creatures die, and we are no exception, but because Christ has been resurrected, we can be sure that this will one day happen to us. Christ has been resurrected first and then all who belong to him will be resurrected when he comes. We cannot know the fine details, and this may be why we are a little uncertain, but we can trust that one day we will be raised.

Pray for those who are bereaved, that they can take strength and comfort from the hope of the resurrection.

MARGOT HODSON

Standing firm in faith

But someone will ask, 'How are the dead raised? With what kind of body...?' How foolish!... When you sow, you do not plant the body... but just a seed... God gives it a body as he has determined... Not all flesh is the same: people have one kind of flesh, animals have another, birds another and fish another. There are also heavenly bodies and there are earthly bodies; but the splendour of the heavenly bodies is one kind, and the splendour of the earthly bodies is another.

Doctor Who fans will know the suspense as they wait to see who the next Doctor will be. Every now and again the Doctor takes on a new human form. Each time, the new person is still the Doctor, but they are a very new character and look very different.

We might imagine that when Jesus was resurrected, it was a bit like this – but it was very different! His body had clearly undergone change and not everyone recognised him, but he still bore the scars of the crucifixion and, once people realised, they had no doubt that it was truly Jesus.

Paul explains that we cannot know what sort of body we will be given at the resurrection. It will not be the same as our present body (the seed) and yet it will be our body. He points out that humans have different bodies to animals and uses that as an analogy to explain the difference between earthly and heavenly bodies.

We are used to thinking of heaven as 'up there'. In the Bible, it simply is God's kingdom, where he rules. When Christ comes, we will be raised on a renewed earth in heavenly bodies. These will be different from our earthly ones, but we will know them to be ours. The key difference is that they will not wear out and cannot be damaged. They will last for eternity.

Paul ends this chapter by referring to Hosea 13:14: 'Where, O death, is your victory? Where, O death, is your sting?' (1 Corinthians 15:55). One day Jesus will return and his victory will be complete. Because of this we can have confidence, whatever we encounter in our lives today.

'Therefore, my dear brothers and sisters, stand firm. Let nothing move you. Always give yourselves fully to the work of the Lord, because you know that your labour in the Lord is not in vain' (1 Corinthians 15:58).

MARGOT HODSON

If you've enjoyed this set of reflections by **Margot and Martin Hodson**, check out their books published with BRF Ministries, including…

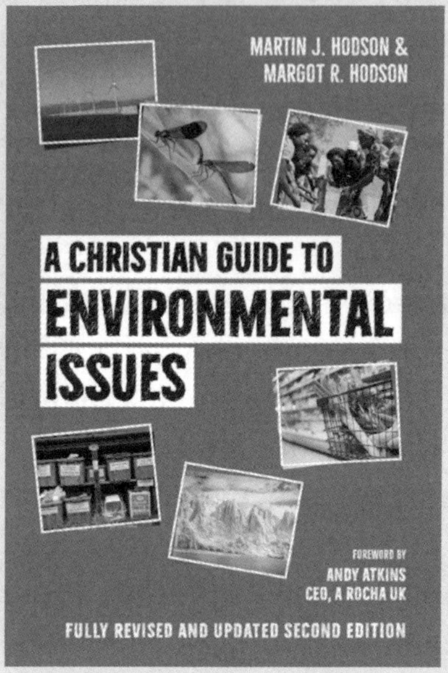

A Christian Guide to Enviromental Issues

978 1 80039 005 8
£9.99

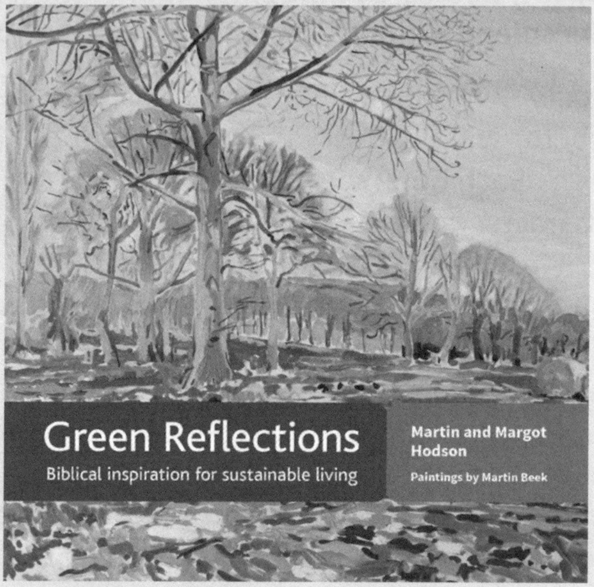

Green Reflections
Biblical inspiration for sustainable living

978 1 80039 068 3
£8.99

To order, visit **brfonline.org.uk** or use the order form at the end.

The supporting cast of the Easter story

As we read again the story of Easter, the story of the death and resurrection of Jesus, there are probably many of the cast with whom we are familiar. For example, Peter and Judas, key players in the narrative, whose lives are dramatically impacted by their response to and the part they played in this pivotal moment in history.

Yet what about the others? What about the supporting cast whose names are given a passing mention on the way to the main event? Real people with real lives that were just as turned upside down by this man Jesus, who had come and walked and lived among them.

What about Malchus, the high priest's servant whose ear was cut off by Peter? Or Pilate's wife, who warned her husband that Jesus was innocent? The Roman centurion and his fellow soldiers who nailed Jesus to the cross? There are a good number who do not take centre stage as the protagonists in the Easter story, but who were there and whose lives were equally impacted by the life, death and resurrection of Jesus.

This week we will turn the spotlight on to some of this supporting cast. We will give airtime to those whose stories often do not get told – one man who was in the wrong place at the wrong time (or maybe it was the right place and right time); two secret followers who step out of the shadows; a pair of weary travellers who had given up hope, only to find themselves surprised by joy; and a heartbroken friend who gets to share the best one-sentence sermon ever spoken, 'He is not dead, he is alive!'

As we look afresh at these lesser-known, often overlooked characters in the most wonderful story ever told, may we know something more of the significant impact of Christ on all of us today. May we, like them, know that every unseen act of devotion, every quiet courageous risk and every unspoken heartbreak and disappointment is held within the heart of the one who conquered death and rose again, that we too may have that eternal hope.

RUTH HASSALL

Carry your cross: Simon of Cyrene

A certain man from Cyrene, Simon, the father of Alexander and Rufus, was passing by on his way in from the country, and they forced him to carry the cross. They brought Jesus to the place called Golgotha... Then they offered him wine mixed with myrrh, but he did not take it. And they crucified him. Dividing up his clothes, they cast lots to see what each would get. It was nine in the morning when they crucified him.

The first of the characters to take to the stage this week is Simon of Cyrene. Simon occupies just one verse in the passion narrative, yet is named and remembered throughout time for the role he played. It is a role he did not choose, and one he might have missed had he left home just ten minutes earlier or later.

We are not told a huge amount about him other than that he was from the North African city of Cyrene – possibly born there, but at the very least a resident – and that he was father to Alexander and Rufus, evidently known within the community of the followers of Jesus. It is thought that he had come to Jerusalem for the Passover, and had found himself, like many others, unable to find accommodation within the city, so was forced to stay in an outlying village.

Earlier in Mark's gospel (8:34), Jesus had told his disciples that following him would require them to deny themselves and carry their cross, giving up their lives in order to truly find life. As Simon made his way to join the celebrations, little did he know just how much that would become a lived reality for him. Taking the road into Jerusalem, he comes across the gathered crowds watching Jesus stagger under the weight of the cross – and before he knows what is happening he is grabbed by the soldiers and forced to carry it. What an incredible paradox – to be carrying the cross of the one who would shortly carry his, and the rest of humanity's, sin on that tree.

We may not be asked to carry the physical cross as Simon did, but Jesus' exhortation holds true for us today.

Living Lord, thank you for taking on my sin.
Help me to take up my cross and follow you. Amen.

RUTH HASSALL

Courageous devotion: Joseph of Arimathea

Now there was a man named Joseph, a member of the Council, a good and upright man, who had not consented to their decision and action. He came from the Judean town of Arimathea, and he himself was waiting for the kingdom of God. Going to Pilate, he asked for Jesus' body. Then he took it down, wrapped it in linen cloth and placed it in a tomb cut in the rock, one in which no one had yet been laid.

Sometimes the need for courage shows itself in the most unexpected places. Joseph of Arimathea discovered this when the two worlds of his work and his devotion collided. Joseph is mentioned only briefly in each of the four gospels, yet we are able to gather a fair bit of information about him – he is a prominent member of the council, a good, upright and, quite likely, rich man.

Up until Jesus' death, Joseph of Arimathea had been a secret follower of Jesus because he feared those in leadership despite earnestly waiting for the kingdom of God to be revealed. Finding himself present but powerless in the meeting of the Sanhedrin where it was decided to present Jesus to Pilate for trial, he watches on in distress as Jesus is condemned and then crucified. The other members of the council had been determined to put an end to Jesus' ministry, and all his arguments in Jesus' defence went unheard.

Joseph knew that unless someone took action, Jesus' body would simply be thrown into a mass grave, so he steps out of the shadows and requests a rare meeting with Pilate to gain permission to take him to a place of burial – the one he had prepared as his own resting place.

Putting his fear aside and disregarding what the other leaders may think, Joseph takes Jesus' broken body down from the cross, lovingly wraps him in linen and lays him in the tomb – actions that spoke love and beauty into the horror of the crucifixion. Each Holy Week we remember this beautiful act of courageous devotion – a spark of light in some incredibly dark days.

Lord Jesus, this day, please show me how I can act with courageous devotion to you. Amen.

RUTH HASSALL

Journey of faith: Nicodemus

Nicodemus, who had gone to Jesus earlier and who was one of their own number [the Pharisees], asked, 'Does our law condemn a man without first hearing him to find out what he has been doing?' They replied, 'Are you from Galilee, too? Look into it, and you will find that a prophet does not come out of Galilee'... He [Joseph of Arimathea] was accompanied by Nicodemus, the man who earlier had visited Jesus at night. Nicodemus brought a mixture of myrrh and aloes, about thirty-five kilograms.

Like Joseph of Arimathea, who we met yesterday, Nicodemus is also a member of the Jewish ruling council, the Sanhedrin, and also showed an interest in Jesus. Nicodemus gets mentioned three times in John's gospel, and each time he steps out a bit further on his journey of faith.

The first time we meet Nicodemus (John 3) he comes to Jesus at night, so as not to be seen. He acknowledges that Jesus is a teacher, who he believes has come from God because of the miracles he has performed. Yet Nicodemus is left confused as Jesus tells him that he must be born again to enter into the kingdom of God.

The second time comes during a conversation recorded in John 7, where the Pharisees and the chief priests are plotting to arrest Jesus. Nicodemus steps in and defends him, saying for this to be just, Jesus needs to be given a fair hearing before an arrest can take place.

Then finally we meet him, along with Joseph of Arimathea, preparing Jesus' body for burial – an act that would indicate that somewhere over time, Nicodemus had come to follow Jesus and was prepared now to risk being seen and counted among his followers.

For some, faith in Jesus is found quickly and easily. For others, however, it can be more like the journey that Nicodemus took – a journey of questioning, of being intrigued by the person of Jesus, yet hiding out in the shadows until they are finally able to fully embrace the fullness of his life.

Lord, I pray today for any I know who are seeking you.
Please reveal yourself to them. Amen.

RUTH HASSALL

Surprised by joy: Mary Magdalene

Now Mary stood outside the tomb crying. As she wept, she bent over to look into the tomb and saw two angels in white, seated where Jesus' body had been, one at the head and the other at the foot... She turned round and saw Jesus standing there, but she did not realise that it was Jesus. He asked her, 'Woman, why are you crying? Who is it you are looking for?' Thinking he was the gardener, she said, 'Sir, if you have carried him away, tell me where you have put him, and I will get him.' Jesus said to her, 'Mary'... Mary Magdalene went to the disciples with the news: 'I have seen the Lord!' And she told them that he had said these things to her.

'It is finished!' That is what Jesus had said just two days earlier (John 19:30). His mission – and to those looking on, his life – was finished. So when Mary went to the tomb, it was a journey made without hope. She had gone to anoint his body and to grieve, only to find it was a tomb no longer! The stone was rolled back, the tomb wide open and Jesus' body gone. Mary weeps, heartbroken with grief. Not only had Jesus died, but to add to her unbearable sadness, his body had been taken and she finds herself alone.

In that moment, Jesus utters just one word – 'Mary' – and in the speaking of her name she knows. Her eyes are opened, and she sees who it is that is really in front of her. He is alive, not defeated! Present with her, not gone! From the depths of her darkest grief, the light of hope begins to burn, and everything is forever changed.

I can only imagine the questions that were flowing through her heart and mind, but I also imagine that the encounter with Jesus himself and the testimony of 'I have seen the Lord!' far outweighed her need for answers.

The Easter story continually calls us to invite the life of God, the life that conquered death and overcame sin, to be present in our lives as well.

Risen Lord, may we be surprised by joy this Easter
as your hope comes alive afresh in us. Amen.

RUTH HASSALL

Present hope: Cleopas

Now that same day two of them were going to a village called Emmaus, about seven miles from Jerusalem… As they talked and discussed these things with each other, Jesus himself came up and walked along with them; but they were kept from recognising him. He asked them, 'What are you discussing together as you walk along?' They stood still, their faces downcast… 'About Jesus of Nazareth,' they replied. 'He was a prophet, powerful in word and deed before God and all the people. The chief priests and our rulers handed him over to be sentenced to death, and they crucified him; but we had hoped that he was the one who was going to redeem Israel.'

'We had hoped …' Have three words ever been weightier with disappointment? Cleopas and his companion (possibly his wife), two weary and sad travellers, are making their way out of Jerusalem and away from all that they had seen unfold there, heading towards Emmaus. As they walk, they rehearse over and over all the reasons why they are so downhearted – primarily because Jesus, the one in whom they had put all their hope and dreams, had been brutally killed and along with him all that they had believed in.

As they walk, a stranger joins them and asks them about their sadness. They find it hard to believe that anyone could not know the events of recent days, unaware that they are talking to the only one who truly knows. They talk, not realising that as he opens the scriptures to them, he is actually letting them know that God has always been present with them and is with them in this very moment, that they have been voicing their grief and disappointment in the presence of Jesus.

The travellers urge Jesus to stay and eat with them, and in the breaking of bread their eyes are opened. In the moment that he's revealed, he disappears, yet they know without a doubt who it was that had been with them.

As we walk our paths, with whatever they hold, we too can have the certainty that Jesus comes and walks with us.

Jesus, would you show me today that you are always with me, even when I struggle to see. Amen.

RUTH HASSALL

Mindfulness is not new, and God's people down the centuries have always been encouraged to practise 'the sacrament of the present moment' – that is, to notice God in the events of everyday life and become attentive to that presence. Tony Horsfall explores six Bible stories that describe individuals encountering God, showing how we can learn how to notice the presence of the divine for ourselves. He also unpacks key spiritual practices that anyone can follow, and introduces insights on the awareness of God from influential writers.

Attentive to God
Being aware of God's presence in daily life
Tony Horsfall
978 1 80039 401 8 £9.99
brfonline.org.uk

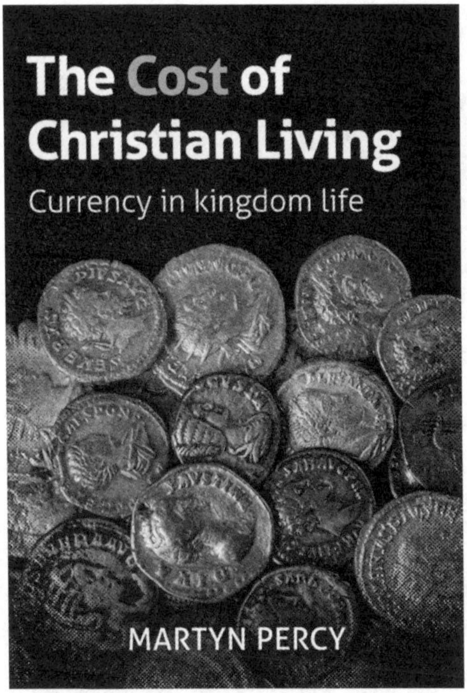

In *The Cost of Christian Living*, Martyn Percy explores the different meanings and uses of money in the gospels. Looking at twelve different stories – parables, miracles and encounters, six from Holy Week and six from elsewhere in the gospels – this book offers a unique perspective on the intersection of faith and finance to help you to engage in a new way with the stories of Jesus' life and death, and to reflect on your own attitudes and choices with regards to money.

The Cost of Christian Living
Currency in kingdom life
Martyn Percy
978 1 80039 349 3 £9.99
brfonline.org.uk

SHARING OUR VISION – MAKING A GIFT

I would like to make a donation to support BRF Ministries. Please use my gift for:

☐ Where the need is greatest ☐ Anna Chaplaincy ☐ BRF Resources
☐ Messy Church ☐ Parenting for Faith

Title	First name/initials	Surname

Address

	Postcode

Email

Telephone

Signature	Date

Please accept my gift of:

☐ £2 ☐ £5 ☐ £10 ☐ £20 Other £ ______

by (*delete as appropriate*):

☐ Cheque/Charity Voucher payable to 'BRF'

☐ MasterCard/Visa/Debit card/Charity card

Name on card

Card no. ☐☐☐☐ ☐☐☐☐ ☐☐☐☐ ☐☐☐☐

Expires end M M Y Y

Signature	Date

Please complete other side of form ➔

SHARING OUR VISION – MAKING A GIFT

BRF Ministries Gift Aid Declaration

In order to Gift Aid your donation, you must tick the box below.

☐ I want to Gift Aid my donation and any donation I make in the future or have made in the past four years to BRF Ministries

I am a UK taxpayer and understand that if I pay less Income Tax and/or Capital Gains Tax in the current tax year than the amount of Gift Aid claimed on all my donations, it is my responsibility to pay any difference.

Please notify BRF Ministries if you want to cancel this Gift Aid declaration, change your name or home address, or no longer pay sufficient tax on your income and/or capital gains.

You can also give online at **brf.org.uk/donate**, which reduces our administration costs, making your donation go further.

Our ministry is only possible because of the generous support of individuals, churches, trusts and gifts in wills.

☐ I would like to leave a gift to BRF Ministries in my will. Please send me further information.

☐ I would like to find out about giving a regular gift to BRF Ministries.

For help or advice regarding making a gift, please contact our fundraising team +44 (0)1235 462305

Your privacy

We will use your personal data to process this transaction. From time to time we may send you information about the work of BRF Ministries that we think may be of interest to you. Our privacy policy is available at **brf.org.uk/privacy**. Please contact us if you wish to discuss your mailing preferences.

Registered with FUNDRAISING REGULATOR

Please complete other side of form

Please return this form to 'Freepost BRF'

No other address information or stamp is needed

Bible Reading Fellowship is a charity (233280) and company limited by guarantee (301324), registered in England and Wales

Overleaf... Reading *New Daylight* in a group | Author profile | Recommended reading | Order and subscription forms

Reading *New Daylight* in a group

GORDON GILES

It is good to talk. While the Rule of Benedict, which formed the spiritual foundations of so many ecclesiastical foundations, recommended daily scripture reading as a key aspect of the community life of work and prayer, during Lent especially each monk was allocated a book to read daily. Benedict's monks did not talk much, but nowadays discussion and reflection can be helpful and enlightening when reading passages that others are simultaneously also reading. Separated by space, as each reads alone, we are yet connected by the common food of scripture, taken in our own time at our own pace. We each chew on it in our own way, and we can all learn from each other's insights and interpretations. To assist with that, here are some open questions that may enable discussion in a Bible study or other group who gather to take further what is published here. The same questions may also aid personal devotion too. Use them as you wish, and may God bless you on your journey as you read, mark and inwardly digest holy words to ponder and nourish the soul

General discussion starters

These can be used for any study series within this issue. There are no right or wrong answers; these questions are simply to enable conversation.

- What do you think is the main idea or theme of the author in this series? Did that come across strongly?
- Have any of the issues discussed touched on personal – or shared – aspects of your life?
- What evidence or stories do the authors draw on to illuminate, or be illuminated by the passages of scripture.
- Which do you prefer: scripture informing daily modern life or modern life shining a new light on scripture?
- Does the author 'call you to action' in a realistic and achievable way? Do you think their ideas will work in the secular world?
- Have any specific passages struck you personally? If so, how and why? Is God speaking to you through scripture and reflection?
- Was anything completely new to you? Any 'eureka' or jaw-dropping moments? If so, what difference will that make?

Questions for discussion

Genesis 1—4 (Martin Leckebusch)

- What aspects of Genesis 1 might have prompted its first readers to worship God the creator, and how do our scientific insights into the complexity of the universe alter our understanding of God?
- From Genesis 1:24—2:7, in what ways are human beings similar to the other land animals, and in what ways are they different?
- How do you understand the commands to 'fill' and 'subdue' the earth, thinking especially about Adam's initial role in the garden?
- In what ways does it matter to have one day a week which is different from the others, and how can that be expressed faithfully and creatively in today's world?
- Think about the choice which Adam and Eve faced in Eden. Would any of us have done better than them at resisting temptation and what does your answer say about being human?
- To what extent can we, as followers of Christ in a broken world, expect to mitigate the ongoing consequences of Adam and Eve's rebellion and the punishment which it incurred?

1 Corinthians 9—11 (Sheila Walker)

- It has been said that the rights of the individual are greatly prized in the developed world, but in many other places they are considered a luxury reserved for the wealthy. As Christians, do we have rights?
- In your own spiritual context, how do you recognise and respond to authority?
- 'Discipline' has been defined as choosing between what I want now and what I want most. How might we learn to hear God in relation to our deepest desires?
- Familiarity can breed if not contempt, then complacency. How might we guard against taking aspects of our faith, or of God, for granted?
- How healthy is the body of Christ where you are? What kind of things will help or hinder its effectiveness?
- What is your understanding and experience of sharing bread and wine together? Why is it important?

Ephesians 3—4 (Roland Riem)

- Does the pattern of Christ's life and death set the pattern for working for reconciliation today?
- In what circumstances can suffering be fruitful for others?
- What is your experience of being 'rooted and grounded in love'?
- How do you manage anger in your community?
- How central to Christian witness and mission is living and working as one body?

The Passover and the second exodus (Gordon Giles)

- Recall the Holy Week and Easter liturgical celebrations you have experienced over the years. How has what has happened in church affected your understanding of the Jewish precedents to the season?
- Has the idea of Jesus' death and resurrection being a 'second exodus' ever occurred to you before? What do you think of the idea? Does the analogy work for you?
- What does it mean when we say, as Paul does, that Jesus is the 'second Adam'?
- Does Holy Communion make more sense when viewed through the lens of the Passover?
- Does the story of the Israelites' oppression under Pharaoh and their subsequent flight have anything to say to us about the plight of migrants and refugees in our age?

Meet the authors: Margot and Martin Hodson

How did you come to faith?

Margot: I came from a Christian family and went to church schools. When I was seven, my school friend told me that Jesus had died for me, and I decided then that I wanted to follow him. My faith deepened at university, where I first began to put faith and environment together.

Martin: My background was secular. As a young scientist, I gained a research fellowship at the Hebrew University in Jerusalem. I decided to try some churches and became a Christian at Christ Church in the Old City.

How did you meet?

Martin: We met in Oxford when Margot came to speak at a day conference – we got talking at lunch and found we had lots in common. Margot was leading a hiking tour in the Negev desert during the following winter, and I booked to go!

What are your current roles?

Margot: We share a teaching ministry with a focus on Christianity and the environment. We teach about science and policy; the theology and ethics; and then how we might respond. Beyond that, Martin is still active in scientific research and currently working on the potential for cereal crops to sequester carbon. I am ordained and give support to my local benefice. I am also a director of the John Ray Initiative, an organisation that seeks to resource the church to respond to the environmental crisis.

What inspires you most?

Martin: We both love nature and walking in the country. In my research, I have sometimes been the first to see something in nature, and I find that totally amazing.

Tell us about working together on writing Bible reading notes.

Margot: We enjoy writing together. With Bible reading notes, we find it helpful to approach a theme together and then divide them between us. Writing can be a very solitary task, so doing the notes together complements our other writing, which is often more individual.

What are your hopes for 2026?

Martin: To say things are not great on the environment would be a massive understatement. We are in the midst of a crisis never before seen by humanity. My hope is that world governments really take it seriously this year and take action.

What Bible character do you find most fascinating?

Margot: I was once asked to preach on Hagar. I'd not really noticed her much before, and I found myself truly respecting her dignity and her deep faith in God. She named her son 'God hears me' (Ishmael) and had a vivid encounter with the angel of the Lord in the desert. I admire her courage in returning to an abusive family situation, and yet that also troubles me. She was treated dreadfully and eventually thrown out of the family home with her son, and both nearly died in the desert. Despite all that, her faith remained strong and God protected her.

Recommended reading

The idea of 'giving something up for Lent' is widely known and discussed today, yet how many know that the ancient discipline of the Lenten fast had several purposes? It was designed as a reminder of our daily dependence on God for all our needs, to draw us closer to God in prayer, to reconnect with the idea of community, and to help us follow Christ's journey through the wilderness and on to Jerusalem. How many of us simply abstain from some treat or other for a few weeks and fail to engage with this deeper meaning of Lent?

This book shows how Lent can be a time for exploring a different kind of 'giving up', one that can transform our lives. In a series of daily studies, Maggi Dawn shows how, throughout scripture, people were radically changed by encountering the true God. If we follow their examples, we can allow the Holy Spirit to shed his light on our ideas of God that are too harsh, too small, too fragile, or too stern.

The following is an edited extract taken from Ash Wednesday, reflecting on Psalm 103:8–18.

I have mixed feelings about the Ash Wednesday liturgy. The ashes from which the day gets its name are made by burning the palm crosses from the previous year's Palm Sunday. During a service of Holy Communion, the fine grey ash is mixed with a little oil and pressed in the shape of the cross on to the forehead of each worshipper with a reminder that, in the words of Genesis 3:19, 'for dust you are and to dust you will return' (NIV). The ashing ritual is a symbol of the fact that we are quite literally made of stardust – the billion-year-old carbon from burnt-out stars, as Joni Mitchell sang in the 1970s.

Lent is partly about the recognition of our own humanity, but the words 'dust to dust' put us squarely in the same territory as a funeral service. Such a baldly punishing declaration of sinfulness can make it hard to see the overriding sense of redemption that the gospel should always carry – so much so that sometimes preachers have been known to downplay the severity of it, and speak of healing our wounds instead of forgiving our sins. Acknowledging both the sinful nature of humanity and our own particular flaws may be essential if we are to escape the arrogance that makes the human heart leaden and ugly. But there is a fine line to tread between avoiding the issue and an over-emphasis on sinfulness that turns the redemptive message of the gospel into the straitjacket of religiosity. How can ashes be redemptive, in any sense of the word?

I think, in fact, that a certain lightness emerges precisely from the process of facing down our own demons. When we look our mortality in the face, the inevitability of our own death asks of us: 'What are you going to do with the life you have?' Years ago I attended the funeral of a friend of mine, who was known to all his friends simply as 'Fairnie'. He was a remarkable and talented man who died suddenly and unexpectedly. I was unprepared for the blow, not only of losing a friend, but of facing the fact that young people – people like me – could just be gone from this world, overnight and without warning. The shock of his death was intensified by the sharp realisation that my own life was far more fragile than I had thought, and the resulting mix of grief and disbelief left me feeling in a slightly dream-like state for some weeks to come.

The huge church where Fairnie's funeral was held was packed with maybe a thousand or more friends and colleagues from widely different contexts, and it gradually became apparent that many of them knew him within their own little world, without having any idea of the breadth of his influence elsewhere. His art students were there, as were a number of high-profile members of the music industry; there were leading members of various denominations, and large contingents from various Christian festivals and communities to which he had contributed. In place of a traditional sermon, tributes and eulogies were given by people who had known him in all these different contexts, and all over the church you could see people's faces lighting up in wonder as they registered the extent of his gifts and achievements. After the funeral was over, tea was served by a group of women from the church, and one of them confided to me in a slightly awe-struck tone: 'We had no idea that he knew all these people. We just thought of him as the college teacher from around the corner.'

In the midst of grief, one of Fairnie's parting gifts to his friends was the realisation that we had no idea how long we had to live, either. All the things I had thought I might do one day suddenly seemed a little more urgent. Not only that, but the breadth of his interests seemed to give permission to flout the cultural wisdom that you can only really do one thing. That day I consciously picked up his Renaissance attitude to life and decided that if I couldn't decide between theology, art and music, I would do them all. Later that year I went to university to take the degree I'd never taken, made another album in my spare time, started writing books and articles, and just for fun I began painting again – something I had let lie dormant for years.

Despite his many gifts, though, Fairnie wasn't focused on achieving things. He always had time for people. I cannot count the times he would just stop for a ten-minute chat, and he knew how to get under the skin of a situation enough to find out what was really going on. He always left you feeling six inches taller, and that bit more capable of living your life. Knowing him left me with the certainty that you should find out what you're good at and do it as much as you can, but also that life is not about creating your personal empire, but about the community you build.

Pausing to contemplate our mortality on Ash Wednesday is not supposed to make us feel bleak, but to startle us into an awareness of the gift of life. We are neither perfect nor immortal: we are merely human, and yet wonderfully made, and we need to know who we are in our imperfections as well as our gifts in order to live every day as if it counts for something. The call to repentance is not a morbid obsession with our failings, but a call to turn away decisively from what keeps us from God, alienates us from other people, and stops us from living well. Lent begins with a challenge to clear out the mental and spiritual clutter, and so discover how to live life to the full.

To order a copy of this book, please use the order form or visit **brfonline.org.uk**

To order

Online: **brfonline.org.uk**
Telephone: +44 (0)1865 319700
Mon–Fri 9.30–17.00

Delivery times within the UK are normally 15 working days. Prices are correct at the time of going to press but may change without prior notice.

Title	Price	Qty	Total
A Christian Guide to Environmental Issues (second edition)	£9.99		
Green Reflections	£8.99		
Attentive to God	£9.99		
To Hell's Mouth and Back	£9.99		
The Cost of Christian Living	£9.99		
Growing in Prayer	£9.99		
Giving It Up (BRF Lent book)	£9.99		

POSTAGE AND PACKING CHARGES			
Order value	**UK**	**Europe**	**Rest of world**
Under £7.00	£2.00	Available on request	Available on request
£7.00–£29.99	£3.00		
£30.00 and over	FREE		

Total value of books	
Postage and packing	
Donation*	
Total for this order	

* Please complete and return the Gift Aid declaration on page 144.

Please complete in BLOCK CAPITALS

Title ________ First name/initials ________________ Surname ________________________________

Address ____

____ Postcode ________________

Acc. No. ________________________ Telephone ________________________________

Email ____

Method of payment

❑ Cheque (made payable to BRF) ❑ MasterCard / Visa

Card no. ☐☐☐☐ ☐☐☐☐ ☐☐☐☐ ☐☐☐☐

Expires end M M Y Y

We will use your personal data to process this order. From time to time we may send you information about the work of BRF Ministries. Please contact us if you wish to discuss your mailing preferences. Our privacy policy is available at **brf.org.uk/privacy**.

Please return this form to:
BRF Ministries, 15 The Chambers, Vineyard, Abingdon OX14 3FE | **enquiries@brf.org.uk**
For terms and cancellation information, please visit **brfonline.org.uk/terms**.

Bible Reading Fellowship (BRF) is a charity (233280) and company limited by guarantee (301324), registered in England and Wales

BRF Ministries needs you!

If you're one of our many thousands of regular *New Daylight* readers you will know all about the impact that regular Bible reading has your faith and the value of daily notes to guide, inform and inspire you. Here are some recent comments from *New Daylight* readers:

> *'Thank you for all the many inspiring writings that help so much when things are tough.'*
>
> *'Just right for me – I learned a lot!'*
>
> *'We looked forward to each day's message as we pondered each passage and comment.'*

If you have similarly positive things to say about *New Daylight*, would you be willing to share your experience with others? Perhaps you could give a short talk or write a brief article about why you find *New Daylight* so helpful. You could form a *New Daylight* reading group, perhaps supplying members with their first copy of the notes. Or you could pass on your back copies or give someone a gift subscription. However you do it, the important thing is to find creative ways to put a copy of *New Daylight* into someone else's hands.

It doesn't need to be complicated and we can help with group and bulk-buy discounts.

We can supply further information if you need it and and would love to hear about it if you do find ways to get *New Daylight* into new readers' hands.

For more information:

- Email **enquiries@brf.org.uk**
- Phone us on **+44 (0)1865 319700** Mon–Fri 9.30–17.00
- Write to us at BRF Ministries, 15 The Chambers, Vineyard, Abingdon OX14 3FE

Inspiring people of all ages to grow in Christian faith

At BRF Ministries, we long for people of all ages to grow in faith and understanding of the Bible. That's what all our work as a charity is about.

- Our range of **BRF Resources** helps Christians go deeper in their understanding of scripture, in prayer and in their walk with God. Our conferences and events bring people together to share this journey, while our Holy Habits resources help whole congregations grow together as disciples of Jesus, living out and sharing their faith.
- We also want to make it easier for local churches to engage effectively in ministry and mission – by helping them bring new families into a growing relationship with God through **Messy Church** or by supporting churches as they nurture the spiritual life of older people through **Anna Chaplaincy**.
- Our **Parenting for Faith** team coaches parents and others to raise God-connected children and teens, and enables churches to fully support them.

Do you share our vision?

Though a significant proportion of BRF Ministries' funding is generated through our charitable activities, we are dependent on the generous support of individuals, churches and charitable trusts.

If you share our vision, would you help us to enable even more people of all ages to grow in faith? Your prayers and financial support are vital for the work that we do. You could:

- support us with a regular donation or one-off gift
- consider leaving a gift to BRF Ministries in your will
- encourage your church to support us as part of your church's giving to home mission – perhaps focusing on a specific ministry or programme
- most important of all, support us with your prayers.

Donate at **brf.org.uk/donate** or use the form on pages 143–44.

A friend indeed

'I no longer call you servants, because a servant does not know his master's business. Instead, I have called you friends, for everything that I learned from my Father I have made known to you. You did not choose me, but I chose you and appointed you so that you might go and bear fruit – fruit that will last – and so that whatever you ask in my name the Father will give you.'

JOHN 15:15–16 (NIV)

In this verse Jesus is speaking to his disciples in the upper room, a farewell and a sending out, words of comfort and empowerment to get them through the coming days. Here he makes it explicit, those gathered in the room are his friends. Their relationship has transcended that of master and servant through the sharing of knowledge. For a servant simply follows the orders of the master while a friend with profound understanding can take initiative and carry ideas forward – and ultimately bear lasting fruit.

For over 100 years, BRF Ministries has been working to share the knowledge of the gospel with as many people of all ages as possible – from BRF Resources, such as our *New Daylight* Bible reading notes, to the work of our other ministries: Anna Chaplaincy, Messy Church and Parenting for Faith. It is our goal not only to share the Bible but to give people the tools for deeper understanding and for building a friendship with God that they can then take forward and, in their own lives and communities, bear fruit.

Our work is made possible through kind donations from individuals, charitable trusts and gifts in wills. If you would like to support our work you can become a Friend of BRF Ministries by making a monthly gift of £2 or more – we thank you for your friendship.

Find out more at **brf.org.uk/donate** or get in touch with us on **01235 462305** or via **giving@brf.org.uk**.

We thank you for your support and your prayers.

The fundraising team at BRF Ministries

Give. Pray. Get involved.
brf.org.uk

NEW DAYLIGHT SUBSCRIPTION RATES

Please note our new subscription rates, current until 30 April 2027:

Individual subscriptions
covering 3 issues for under 5 copies, payable in advance (including postage & packing):

	UK	Europe	Rest of world
New Daylight	£25.50	£37.50	£44.25
New Daylight Deluxe per set of 3 issues p.a.	£30.15	£45.15	£61.05

Group subscriptions
covering 3 issues for 5 copies or more, sent to one UK address (post free):

New Daylight	£17.97 per set of 3 issues p.a.
New Daylight Deluxe	£21.75 per set of 3 issues p.a.

Please note that the annual billing period for group subscriptions runs from 1 May to 30 April.

Overseas group subscription rates
Available on request. Please email **enquiries@brf.org.uk**.

Copies may also be obtained from Christian bookshops:

New Daylight	£5.99 per copy
New Daylight Deluxe	£7.25 per copy

All our Bible reading notes can be ordered online by visiting **brfonline.org.uk/subscriptions**

NEW DAYLIGHT INDIVIDUAL SUBSCRIPTION FORM

All our Bible reading notes can be ordered online by visiting
brfonline.org.uk/subscriptions

Title __________ First name/initials ____________ Surname ______________________________

Address ____

____ Postcode ____________________

Telephone _________________________ Email ___________________________________

Please send ***New Daylight*** beginning with the May 2026 / September 2026 / January 2027 issue (*delete as appropriate*):

(*please tick box*)	**UK**	**Europe**	**Rest of world**
New Daylight	☐ £25.50	☐ £37.50	☐ £44.25
New Daylight Deluxe	☐ £30.15	☐ £45.15	☐ £61.05

Optional donation to support the work of BRF Ministries £ ________________

Total enclosed £ _________________ (cheques should be made payable to 'BRF')

Please complete and return the Gift Aid declaration on page 144 to make your donation even more valuable to us.

Please charge my MasterCard / Visa with £ ________________

Card no. ☐☐☐☐ ☐☐☐☐ ☐☐☐☐ ☐☐☐☐

Expires end M M Y Y

We will use your personal data to process this order. From time to time we may send you information about the work of BRF Ministries. Please contact us if you wish to discuss your mailing preferences. Our privacy policy is available at **brf.org.uk/privacy**.

Please return this form with the appropriate payment to:
BRF Ministries, 15 The Chambers, Vineyard, Abingdon OX14 3FE
For terms and cancellation information, please visit **brfonline.org.uk/terms**.

Bible Reading Fellowship is a charity (233280) and company limited by guarantee (301324), registered in England and Wales

NEW DAYLIGHT GIFT SUBSCRIPTION FORM

☐ I would like to give a gift subscription (please provide both names and addresses):

Title ____________ First name/initials ______________ Surname ______________________________

Address ____

____ Postcode ____________________

Telephone ____________________________ Email _____________________________________

Gift subscription name ____

Gift subscription address ____

____ Postcode ____________________

Gift message (20 words max. or include your own gift card):

____

____

Please send ***New Daylight*** beginning with the May 2026 / September 2026 / January 2027 issue (*delete as appropriate*):

(*please tick box*)	**UK**	**Europe**	**Rest of world**
New Daylight	☐ £25.50	☐ £37.50	☐ £44.25
New Daylight Deluxe	☐ £30.15	☐ £45.15	☐ £61.05

Optional donation to support the work of BRF Ministries £ ____________________

Total enclosed £ ____________________ (cheques should be made payable to 'BRF')

Please complete and return the Gift Aid declaration on page 144 to make your donation even more valuable to us.

Please charge my MasterCard / Visa with £ __________________

Card no. ☐☐☐☐ ☐☐☐☐ ☐☐☐☐ ☐☐☐☐

Expires end M M Y Y

We will use your personal data to process this order. From time to time we may send you information about the work of BRF Ministries. Please contact us if you wish to discuss your mailing preferences. Our privacy policy is available at **brf.org.uk/privacy**.

Please return this form with the appropriate payment to:
BRF Ministries, 15 The Chambers, Vineyard, Abingdon OX14 3FE
For terms and cancellation information, please visit **brfonline.org.uk/terms**.